# BECOMING AN ENTREPRENEUR

## How to Find Freedom and Fulfillment as a Business Owner

by Jake Desyllas

# BECOMING AN ENTREPRENEUR

The Voluntary Life Press
Unit 310, 91 Western Road, Brighton BN1 2NW
United Kingdom


Becoming an Entrepreneur: How to Find Freedom and Fulfillment as a Business Owner

Jake Desyllas

Copyright © Jake Desyllas, 2014


First Published in the United Kingdom by The Voluntary Life Press, 2014

ISBN-13: 978-1500242411
ISBN-10:1500242411


Copyeditor: Cheryl Hulsapple
Cover & book design: Will Moyer

# Contents

Introduction

1

Chapter One - Breaking Free

9

Chapter Two - Something People Want

21

Chapter Three - You Provide the Purpose

33

Chapter Four - Learn by Selling

47

Chapter Five - The Unexamined Business Is Not Worth Building

61

Chapter Six - The Best Funding There Is

75

Chapter Seven - Make Yourself Redundant

91

Chapter Eight - Profit Is Sanity

103

Chapter Nine - JFDI (Just Fucking Do It)

115

Further Resources

125

Further Reading

127

Acknowledgements

131

About the Author

135

*For Hannah, with all my love.*

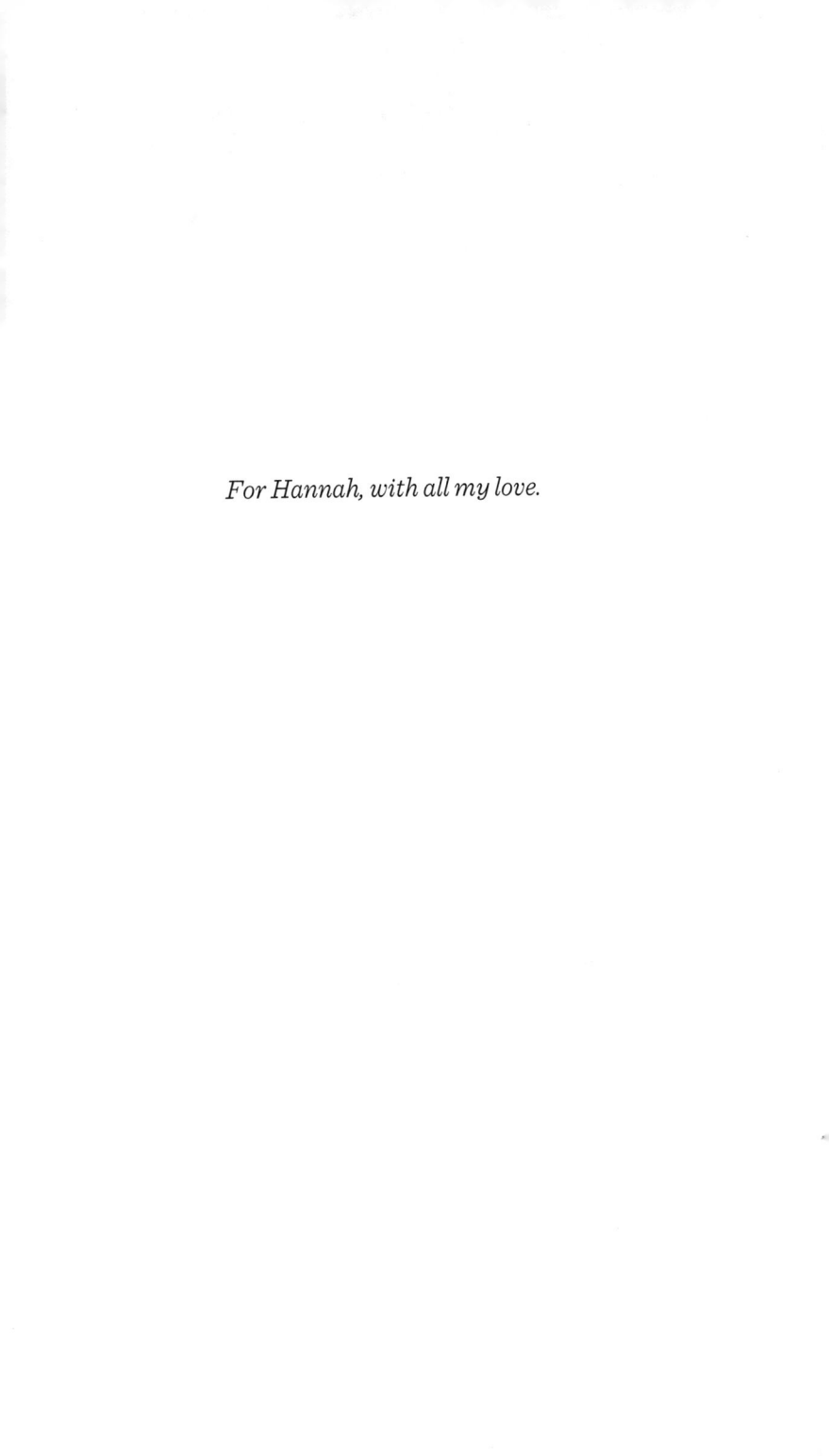

# Introduction

Becoming an entrepreneur fundamentally changed my view on how to achieve freedom and fulfillment. Starting a business is the most liberating act that you can undertake in your life. It's a peak experience that will change you forever, regardless of the outcome.

Entrepreneurship gave me the freedom to live every day as I choose. It enabled me to master challenges that once scared me. It gave me the opportunity to dedicate myself to work that is truly meaningful to me. For a long time, that work involved founding, growing, and finally selling my own business. Today, the work that is most meaningful to me is helping others to free themselves through entrepreneurship.

I don't come from an entrepreneurial family. For most of my childhood, I lived in a communal squat in South London. The adults that I learned from were employees, not business owners. I grew up in a political atmosphere at home and school in which people were suspicious of business; I was taught the word "capitalist"—as a pejorative—at least a decade before I learned the word "entrepreneur." I spent years in college and postgraduate research before it even occurred to me that I could start my own business.

Like most people, I learned nothing in school about entrepreneurship. I wasn't even aware that it was a viable option. I got the same message from school that I heard from my parents: the key to a good life is a good job, and the key to getting a good job is getting good grades.

Nonetheless, deep down I knew that I never wanted to work for anyone else. The prospect of spending life as an employee seemed like such a drag. I believed that it must be possible to do something more fulfilling with my life than working for other people, even though I didn't know what that would be.

As I experimented with different kinds of work and postgraduate study, I could see people of my own age founding businesses in the first wild wave of Internet startups during the boom years of the 1990s. I saw people of my generation grow and sell their businesses and retire early to do whatever they wanted with their days. That all looked like awesome fun. They didn't seem smarter than me, so I figured if they could do it, I could do it too.

I became an entrepreneur at the age of twenty-eight, when I created a startup called "Intelligent Space" with one business partner. We defined Intelligent Space as a *pedestrian movement consultancy*. Our goal was to help architects, engineers, and property developers make the world a better place for pedestrians. Pedestrian flows are the lifeblood to the economy of cities: they are vital to all face-to-face retail. The presence or absence of people on foot can make a city street either a place that you want to be in, or one that feels dangerous. At the time, there were very few tools available to assist architects and developers in creating pedestrian-friendly designs.

We developed computer simulations that mapped where people are likely to walk, which is often not the same as where architects or engineers think they *should* walk. We used science-based methods to turn pedestrian movement from an undervalued resource into a tangible and manageable asset. I was aware that the designs of many buildings and streets were terribly dysfunctional for pedestrians, and I saw an opportunity to help improve urban designs through the simulation of pedestrian flows.

After starting the business, I began to realize how little I understood about entrepreneurship and how many mistakes I was making. I had technical skill, but I did not understand how to provide a service that was helpful. I had a lot of drive, but I wasn't clear about the purpose of my business. I avoided selling to clients because it was uncomfortable, even though it was the most important thing to do. I didn't have systems in place to track and analyze how my business was performing, so I didn't know about many problems until it was too late. I worked ridiculously long hours. Day-to-day operations were still very dependent on me, so I did a lot of work that I could have delegated.

Because I didn't know what I was doing, the growth of my company was unsustainable. In the first year, we spent a lot of money on things that we didn't need, like the rental of a nice office. We had to cut back and fire people shortly after we completed our first big project because we didn't have any new projects lined up. I took on large debts to fund my business. I was personally on the hook for over

£150,000 (approximately $246,000) in loans. It was the biggest risk I had ever taken and after two years, it did not look good.

My education had trained me for life as a reliable employee and taught me nothing of what I needed to know to run a business. I was just making it up as I went along, and that wasn't working. I needed conscious principles to follow in making decisions about my business. I resolved to learn everything that I could about entrepreneurship and to start running the business in a more principled way as fast as I could. I read voraciously, paid for business coaching, and did a lot of rethinking.

As I implemented what I was learning, the business went from one that lacked clear direction to a highly transparent and systematic operation. Intelligent Space became a very successful consultancy. It took five years to pay off the initial loans and achieve profitability. We continued to grow revenue and increase our profit margin, until we sold the business to a multinational engineering company in a trade-sale two years later.

In the end, my little startup had a clearer purpose, more transparent business controls, and a higher profit rate than the huge multinational company that bought us. I worked as a director in the multinational company for three years, as part of an earn-out agreement. Then I retired early, at the age of thirty-eight.

## About This Book

This book is for you if you want to become an

entrepreneur, or if you already are one and want more freedom and fulfillment. I've set out the principles that helped me directly in becoming a successful entrepreneur. Although I use examples from my experience in starting a consultancy, the principles that I discuss in the book are true for any industry.

I've tried to express these ideas as simply as possible, avoiding technical language wherever possible. You don't need much background knowledge of business in order to understand the contents. I've drawn from a wide variety of sources, especially from other entrepreneurs. If you are interested in reading more about the principles that I adopted, you can find references in the footnotes and suggestions for further reading at the end of the book.

In a nutshell, these were my guiding principles:

**Be helpful. Make something people want.** I hold a BA Honors (first class), an MSc (with distinction), and a PhD. It was humbling to realize that such things are largely irrelevant in business. What counts is one's ability to be helpful and make something that people want. This is what Chapter Two - Something People Want is about.

**Provide purpose.** I started the business with only a vague idea of what I was doing. I came to understand that my most important responsibility was to provide a defining purpose and a clear vision for the venture. This is the subject of Chapter Three - You Provide the Purpose.

**Learn by selling.** Although selling our services to potential customers was the last thing I wanted to do at first, I came to understand that it was the most important activity for my business. Chapter Four - Learn by Selling explains how selling is the mechanism through which you learn to shape your business for the better.

**Measure everything.** When I started my business, I was running from one emergency to the next. After my rethink, I adopted a very proactive approach to tracking and analysis. This is the subject of Chapter Five - The Unexamined Business Is Not Worth Building.

**Don't spend it until you've got it**. I learned (the hard way) that spending money until you run out is not a good plan. Instead, I came to adopt the approach of funding the business from earnings. This is the subject of Chapter Six - The Best Funding There Is.

**Make yourself redundant.** I learned to stop increasing my responsibilities within the business and do the opposite: extract myself from workflows as much as possible. This concept is explained in Chapter Seven - Make Yourself Redundant.

**Revenue is vanity and profit is sanity.** Instead of focusing on growth, I learned to focus on what matters for the health of the business: profit. This is the subject of Chapter Eight - Profit Is Sanity.

**Act despite uncertainties.** I had to give myself permission to risk failure, in order to achieve something remarkable. This is the subject of Chapter Nine - JFDI (Just Fucking Do It).

I did not adopt all these principles uniformly. In fact, I became conscious of them partly because of the mistakes I made when I didn't apply them. In struggling to become a better entrepreneur, I realized that my education and upbringing had all been geared towards becoming a lifelong employee. This is a very common experience, and it represents one of the biggest challenges to anyone starting their own business. Chapter One - Breaking Free is about overcoming your conditioning in order to make it as an entrepreneur.

I encourage you to get in touch with me and tell me what you think about the ideas in this book. I'd love to hear about your experiences with finding freedom and fulfillment through entrepreneurship. If you have constructive suggestions on how I can improve the book and make it more helpful, I'd love to hear them too. You can email me at jake@thevoluntarylife.com.

Jake Desyllas

Puerto Vallarta, Mexico, February 2014

CHAPTER ONE
# Breaking Free

*Perfect freedom is reserved for the man who lives by his own work and, in that work, does what he wants to do.*

—R. G. Collingwood

Entrepreneurship provides the best opportunity for anyone to experience the three most fulfilling *intrinsic* motivations[1] in life: purpose, mastery and autonomy.

**Purpose** is the motivation that comes from having an important reason for whatever you do. It is the conviction that what you're doing matters. Your work means something significant to you. You have the satisfaction of knowing that you are doing something useful with your life and that your work has value in the world.

**Mastery** is the motivation that comes from a desire to achieve a high level of skill, control, and self-expression through what you do. It is the sense that you're involved in work that enables you to gain a greater sense of effectiveness, and consequently, greater self-esteem. Everything you do when starting your own business is a chance at mastery. The entrepreneurial skills that I found hardest to master were also those that became the most rewarding: learning how to sell, learning how to create a working enterprise, and learning how to make a profit.

**Autonomy** is the motivation that comes from wanting the freedom to do what *you* think is best with your life, not what anyone else thinks. Entrepreneurship is the only opportunity to seek financial freedom—the freedom *not* to work on anything that you don't enjoy—that is open to anyone. This is the most genuine sense of freedom that you can experience.

As an entrepreneur, you alone determine your goals. You have the opportunity to master your own challenges. You have the maximum freedom possible in what you do. Your own efforts lead to your own achievements and rewards. Entrepreneurship is an opportunity to live a purposeful life, without regrets. It is the freest and most fulfilling way of life I know.

## Self-Liberation for Everyone

This is a program for self-liberation available to everyone. You do not have to have a particular personality type to succeed in creating your own business. There are successful introvert entrepreneurs, as well as extroverts. There are those who prefer to persuade, as well as those who like to direct. There are detail-oriented people, as well as those who are best at seeing the big picture. Each person can create a business in his or her own way.

Customers don't care which school you went to or which exams you passed. They don't care about the race, gender or sexual orientation of the entrepreneur behind a business. They simply care about whether your product is useful to them.

There is no limit to the number of people who can start their own business at any one time. It's not as if there are only so many entrepreneur "jobs" available. Humans will never run out of unfulfilled needs for businesses to meet, so anyone can invent a business that will be relevant to some market.

We could live in a world of entrepreneurs. *Everyone* could work for themselves—in a vast network of independent contractors. Perhaps we are moving towards that possible future. I believe we would all be far happier and more responsible for it. Everyone would gain an understanding of basic economics and the importance of reciprocity. The world could be unimaginably more peaceful and prosperous as a result.

The opportunity to start your own business is one of the great privileges of our times. I'm thankful that I was born in this period of great business creativity and development after the Industrial Revolution, and not during the vast majority of earlier history when most entrepreneurs were killed for upsetting the existing order. It's up to us to take advantage of the possibilities that this time offers.

Even within my lifetime, technological change has made it far easier to become an entrepreneur. It is now feasible to start your own business over a weekend and have access to a truly global market on Monday.

The technology available to us would have astonished any entrepreneur working even one generation ago. We have frictionless access to any customer or supplier on earth through the Internet. We can use crowdfunding to raise money without being beholden to powerful institutions. We have real-time reporting systems that show how our businesses are performing. We can use a huge selection of cheap automation tools to scale our businesses easily.

## What Holds People Back

Here is a strange contradiction of our times: although it has never been easier to be an entrepreneur, nearly everyone is trained to become an employee. Most people are indoctrinated from an early age to imagine that the only realistic option for supporting themselves is getting a job. They learn to think like worker drones and to spend their lives following directions from someone else. It's a kind of *employee* conditioning.

Most people become so indoctrinated that they assume, by default, that they need to *get a job* from an employer in order to make a living. As children, they were taught that passing exams—obtaining certification from someone else—is the key to finding a "good job." In contrast, when you start a business, you *create* opportunities for yourself and others, by finding new ways to be helpful.

Employee conditioning creates the mentality of followers. The default assumption is that somebody else makes the big decisions and your job is to follow them. However, as an entrepreneur, you are your own leader. You have an exciting opportunity to provide a defining *purpose* for your ventures.

Most people have been trained to look to authority figures for rewards. They look to bosses to give them a promotion, just as they were trained as children to look to teachers for grades and to parents for approval. In contrast, an entrepreneur looks for *reciprocation* from customers, as equals, for value provided.

When you think like an employee, you expect someone else to be the judge of your own progress. Your boss gets to decide how you are doing, and you work to influence his perception. In contrast, if you create a business, *you* take responsibility to assess how you are doing.

Employee conditioning shelters you from many of the important questions facing a business owner, such as how to finance a venture. When you are trained to think like an employee, you focus on office politics and miss out on the really interesting decisions facing the business. Most people have no idea about the options available to finance a business and the advantages or disadvantages of each option; I certainly didn't know about such things.

As employees, people think they need to take on more and more responsibility in the work process in order to secure their jobs. Many entrepreneurs are also held back by the conditioning that leads them to take on ever more responsibility. Despite financial success, business owners often suffer from stress and burnout because their business depends on their input for so many aspects of day-to-day operations.

I will suggest a completely different approach: as a

business owner, the most valuable work you can do is to design workflows. The quicker you extract yourself from active involvement in these workflows, the better it will be for you and your business. The employee mentality teaches a goal of finding work and hanging on to it, but your goal as an entrepreneur is to create value and make yourself obsolete in the process. It's a wonderful opportunity to change the way you work.

Employee conditioning trains us to judge and justify our work by effort and intention. We become involved in intricate hierarchical games, whereby employers try to influence our behavior, and we try to beat the system. When you start your own business, you judge everything by results because that's what matters. You do things to make a real impact, not because other people want you to.

As an employee, you are trained to avoid risking failure at the cost of never doing anything extraordinary. Starting a business requires you to risk failure in order to achieve something truly remarkable.

## Why It's Hard

The main reason people find starting a business scary and confusing is that they've been conditioned in their most formative years to think of themselves as employees. Children are natural entrepreneurs: they have a restless curiosity and creativity. Employees are not born; they are made by years of indoctrination.

The most obvious source of employee conditioning is school, where we spend over a decade being prepared for the workplace. The whole point of modern compulsory schooling, as it has evolved since its invention in nineteenth century Prussia, is to make employees out of kids. Some educational luminaries have expressed this quite explicitly. John Dewey wrote; "Every teacher should realize he is a social servant set apart for the maintenance of the proper social order and the securing of the right social growth."[2]

The purpose of schooling is often unclear even to many people working within it. School is a factory for the production of employees. Even the teachers have been conditioned by it. Every single schoolteacher you ever had was an employee. Is it any wonder that they taught *you* to think like one?

School is a kind of prison for kids, and we are all ex-cons trying to find our way in the world outside. School did not just leave us unprepared for starting a business, it made us *less capable* because it trained us to think like employees. If sitting in rows for years at school impressed anything upon us, it was how to think like followers. The person who mattered was the one dispensing knowledge at the front of the class. We were only there to absorb teachings from the leader and to try to gain their favor.

A less obvious source of employee conditioning is the family. The model of being an employee and having a boss is very familiar to many people because most parents behave like the bosses of their children (and crappy bosses, to boot). They use punishment and rewards to get their kids to comply, rather than cultivating a relationship based on negotiation with them. This kind of parenting treats children more like pets to be trained than like individuals whose preferences are respected.

Compliance-oriented parenting leaves people with a deeply hierarchical view of relationships. We learn to take it for granted that someone in charge gives out the orders and everyone else has to comply. This limits our view as adults of what working life can be. We go from one hierarchical job to another, hoping to move up the career ladder, often blind to the opportunity of a life outside the job hierarchy as a business owner.

I hope that someday compulsory schooling—that hangover from the nineteenth century—will end. More people will realize how completely outdated the idea of forced schooling is for the world that we now live in. I also hope there will come a time when the general standard of parenting improves to the point at which children are treated as vulnerable individuals to be negotiated with, rather than as underlings whose job is to comply. However, those of us born before such a time have to unlearn our conditioning in order to be free.

Today it is feasible for anyone who wants to become an entrepreneur to do so; we've just been trained not to try. The employee mindset significantly lags behind the opportunities available today. It's long overdue that we leave our employee conditioning behind. It's amazing how much more joy and fulfillment you can have when you stop thinking like an employee and free yourself to act as an entrepreneur.

## Breaking Free

Some people choose to find comfort in what is familiar to them. If you want to work in jobs, then the employee conditioning that you received might suit you. You can spend your whole life doing that, if you'd like. The problem is this: if you do want to create your own business, this conditioning imprisons your creativity and convinces you that there is no escape from your jobbing lifestyle. I believe that if we weren't all trained to think of ourselves as employees, then nobody these days would want to be one. There is too much fun and fulfillment to be had as an entrepreneur.

Almost everyone who starts their own business has a range of learned prejudices, preoccupations, and bad habits that sabotage their own success—I certainly had mine, as you will see throughout this book. Starting a business pits you against all the messages inside your head that hold you back in life. This is the psychological challenge of entrepreneurship. When you free yourself of this conditioning, you free yourself in life, and you gain fulfillment as an entrepreneur.

The employee mentality is an unhealthy state of mind. It leads you to think that your locus of control is outside yourself. It encourages you to look to others to tell you what to do and think. The fact that this way of thinking is the norm is a sign of how indoctrinated most people are at present.

In contrast, entrepreneurship requires critical thinking expressed in creative action. As Michelangelo put it, you *criticize by creating*. To think like a successful entrepreneur, you simply need to think as a rational individual does. Learning to be an entrepreneur is about unlearning your employee conditioning so that you can think *freely* again. This book will help you dump your employee conditioning, free yourself to take action as an entrepreneur, and have a great time in the process.

Work takes up such a huge proportion of our time, energy, and life. It's far too important to leave it to someone else to decide what your best work can be. If you are willing to take the risk and responsibility of starting your own business, you will have the freedom to do the work that you choose in the way that you want. If you know deep down that you'd find this choice more fulfilling, despite how scary or challenging it might seem, then read on. I'm going to help you stage a prison break.

CHAPTER TWO

# Something People Want

*In a sense there's just one mistake that kills startups: not making something users want.*

—Paul Graham

The way that you prepare for a career as an employee is nothing like the way to prepare for starting a business. The model of preparation for life that I learned was certification: passing exams. This is the idea that you gain access to the next stage of your life by showing various "important people" that you can pass their tests. You pass school exams in order to get into university. You pass your university degree in order to get a job. Many people go on to pass professional exams in order to practice a restricted profession. I was very embedded within this approach: I got a bachelor's degree, a master's degree, and a doctorate.

This is fundamentally the employee way of thinking: the jobs are out there, pre-made. Your path to obtaining a job is also predefined, as certification. Your task is to adapt yourself to fit one of these predefined paths to a pre-made job. School conditions us into the mindset of training for a "career" comprising such jobs. Career guidance counsellors, themselves lifelong employees, give advice about particular jobs for which, supposedly, you would be well-suited. The underlying premise is that you are destined to go and *get a job*. This doesn't prepare you for the challenges of *creating your own venture*.

Preparing to become an entrepreneur is a completely different exercise. Potential customers do not issue exams that you can cram for in order to get their business. Nobody cares what school you went to or what degrees you have. What they care about is whether you are doing something that is helpful to them.

Entrepreneurship seemed like an alien way of life to me when I was at university. My vague notions about how to become an entrepreneur tended to be infused with wishful thinking: I thought the key was to have a brilliant idea—that eureka moment of inspiration. However, that is not the most important requirement for starting a business.

What counts for success is not so much your business idea (which will change over time) but rather your capability to *execute* it. You will be more capable of executing some ideas than others, so it helps to be conscious of your own strengths and weakness in choosing what kind of business to start. In this chapter we will review what capabilities you need and identify how to acquire, develop, and master them.

Put simply, your business capability is just your ability to be helpful: to provide value to others in a way that they recognize and appreciate. When you ask yourself what kind of business you should start, what you are really asking is, "What can I do that would be helpful to others?" That is a more practical way of looking at the question.

You need three core capabilities in order to provide value to customers. These are:
1. **Customer empathy**
2. **Industry knowledge**
3. **Technical expertise**

If you have all of these for a particular idea, you're in the best position to start a business in that area. If you have none of them, then you need to develop them first, or see if you can find a different business idea that you have more capability to deliver. If you have one or two, then you know where your strengths and weaknesses lie. Let's look at each of these capabilities in more detail.

## Customer Empathy

You can only help improve customers' lives if you understand them. Customer empathy is the ability to put yourself in a customer's shoes and understand their problems. In order to do this, you need to understand how they live at present and how your proposed offering could improve their lives.

One of the best ways to get good customer empathy is to *be a customer yourself* for whatever solution your business provides. This is known colloquially as "eating your own dog food." It is helpful because you experience the same needs that your customers experience. A business must create value for people. In order for this to happen, the business owner needs to understand what other people want. It's a lot easier to understand what others want if you want the same thing too.

If you personally need the solution that you intend to provide through your business, then you will be a far better judge of whether or not the business is successful at fulfilling the need. This approach informed Steve Jobs's decisions about product development at Apple. He often said that he worked to create products that he would be proud to share with his friends and family and that he personally wanted to use.[3] I applied this approach to the book you are now reading: I wrote about the ideas that I found most helpful and inspiring when I started my business.

If you're building a product or service that you personally need and will continually use, then you are in a good position to make informed decisions about improving, refining, and evolving your product. You will see which changes to the product help you. Phil Libin, CEO of the note-taking application company *Evernote*, talks about how he finds it much easier to run Evernote than the previous companies he founded because he and his team use the product daily. The Evernote developers do immediate market testing on themselves.[4]

However, you might want to start a business offering something for which you're not a potential customer. This is often the case if your product or service is designed to help businesses rather than individual consumers. For example, my pedestrian movement consulting business provided advice to retail developers. Since I had never worked as a retail developer, I was never a potential customer for my service. In other words, I wasn't able to "eat my own dog food."

Entrepreneurs who can't be a customer for their own product rely on research and imagination as tools to develop customer empathy. This means getting as much understanding of your customers as possible in order to simulate within your own mind what it is like to be in their position. This is harder than being a user of your own product, as you need to rely on feedback from your customers. On the other hand, even if you use your product, it still helps enormously to get feedback from paying customers, since they are able to provide you with a more objective assessment of your product or service.

There are many ways of getting structured feedback from customers, from e-mail questionnaires to in-person interviews. I interviewed our customers regularly throughout the growth of my business and asked them for detailed feedback on how we could better meet their needs. Those interviews helped me understand and empathize with them better. The biggest source of customer feedback comes through the sales process itself, which we will discuss more in chapter four.

## Industry Knowledge

You can't be helpful to your customers until you understand their circumstances. Customers do not exist in a vacuum; they are people working and living within their own constraints. Where they live, work, or shop might have a big impact on whether they can buy from you. Perhaps it matters which operating system they use or which devices they own. Maybe it's important to know when they get paid and how much they can spend.

It is also important to understand the circumstances of the other businesses that serve your customers. This could include understanding how potential distributors interact with your customers. It could involve knowing potential affiliates and how to incentivize them. It might also include understanding any major issues in the industry that are changing the way that people do business.

The best source of industry knowledge is previous work in the industry. This kind of knowledge is one of the most valuable things that you can get from any jobs that you have before starting your own business. I worked as a property market consultant before starting my own consultancy, which gave me valuable insights into the problems facing property development companies. You can view your experiences as an employee as great opportunities to get an insider's understanding of a particular industry.

Additionally, you can learn about an industry from having close contact with other people who work in it, such as friends and family. My father is an architect, so I was able to gain insight into how architects purchase consulting services and how they could be partners for our services. It is beneficial to talk to as many people as you can about their work so that you can learn about what happens in their industry.

You can also gain industry knowledge simply by finding resources that teach you about how the industry works.

For example, I didn't know anything about self-publishing when I chose to publish this e-book, so I read books in order to learn about it.

Even if you don't know anyone in the industry, when you reach out to people and ask to talk to them, you may be surprised by how helpful they can be. Most entrepreneurs I know are happy to talk to others who are trying to start a business. They can be a great source of industry knowledge and they may connect you to people with whom you could develop partner or affiliate relationships.

The real value of all this knowledge is to give you an understanding of how money flows around your customers. This will make you more capable of delivering value and getting paid for it. Your empathy for customers will be supported by a practical understanding of their context and constraints.

## Technical Expertise

Technical expertise is specialist knowledge about how to deliver a quality product cost-effectively. This includes knowledge about how to improve quality or reduce cost, without compromising either.

The rarer the technical expertise you have, the harder it will be for customers to get your offering from someone else. If they need the benefits that your product provides and cannot get those benefits elsewhere, then your offering will be valuable.

Technical expertise can give you the opportunity to innovate in ways that increase productivity or improve customer experience. If you know how to do something differently or provide a service that is totally new, it can give you a huge business advantage. This is why entrepreneurs cluster around fast-developing technology: that's where the opportunities are. Fast-developing technologies are risky and uncertain, therefore there is less competition and a bigger potential upside.

Acquiring technical expertise means becoming skilled at something that is both difficult and useful. The starting point for this kind of expertise is to immerse oneself in a chosen subject area and learn all there is to know about it. However, knowing about a subject is only a precondition. The expertise lies in the ability to *do things* with this knowledge; for example: create more beautiful music, code better software, or coach people more effectively. It's not about what you know, it's about what you can *do*.

Developing technical expertise seems similar to the kind of learning undertaken in school or university. For this reason, it is easy to focus on your need for technical expertise at the expense of customer empathy and industry knowledge. Learning techie stuff may feel familiar; at least it did to me. This often translates into a focus on improving the quality of your product or service. The danger is that if you focus on technical issues without sufficient regard to customer empathy or industry knowledge, you will end up making improvements that nobody cares about.

I was conscious about the technical expertise needed for my business, but I was quite unaware of the importance of customer empathy and industry knowledge, so I focused on research and development at the expense of sales. In the first year, I spent a huge amount of time and energy solving the technical problems necessary to get our software to work. I devoted much less time and energy to the vitally important question of what our customers really needed from us.

As well as technical expertise relevant to your specific industry, you also need to develop expertise in the practice of running a business itself. This expertise is totally alien to the employee mentality taught in school. Business expertise involves a range of abilities: to sell, to track operations transparently, to create standardized workflows, and to steer your business towards profitability. We will look in detail at developing these general business skills in later chapters.

## Build Your Advantage

Here are the three important things to remember about preparing for entrepreneurship:

- Choose a venture for which you have great empathy for proposed customers. Ideally, be a customer yourself ("eat your own dog food").
- Develop your industry knowledge by working in the industry, talking to people who understand it, and reading about it.
- Build your technical expertise by developing rare and valuable skills in your proposed area of business.

In the best-case scenario, you will create a business for which you have great customer empathy (perhaps even as a customer for your own product), you will have industry knowledge, and you will have unique technical expertise. However, you probably won't start with all three capabilities. By reviewing the areas where you are weaker, you can identify which capabilities you need in order to start a business and plan how to acquire them.

Developing your capabilities will give you an *information advantage* for entrepreneurship. Prepare yourself so that you have a unique understanding of what your potential customers really want, what their circumstances are, and how to resolve technical problems relating to them. If you understand these things better than most people, then you have an advantage. That is where the value lies.

As the science fiction writer William Gibson said, "The future is already here; it's just unevenly distributed." If you know things in advance of others, you are able to see a little part of one possible future. You can make your vision of the future come true. In order to do so, you need to be conscious of your purpose.

CHAPTER THREE
# You Provide the Purpose

*If you want to build a ship, don't drum up the men to gather wood, divide the work, and give orders. Instead, teach them to yearn for the vast and endless sea.*

—Antoine de Saint-Exupéry

I started a business with only a vague idea of what it was for. I came to understand that my most important responsibility was to provide a clear vision for the venture. The essential element of every successful business is an entrepreneur with an inspiring purpose. The technical details of your business will change and develop throughout the life of the business, but your purpose remains consistent.

We're not taught to think about purpose in this way. The employee mentality is fundamentally a follower mentality. The default assumption is that somebody else makes the big decisions; our job is to follow them. This can lead to a lifetime spent looking for the next boss to follow. It's time we all unlearned our follower conditioning and started thinking for ourselves again. As entrepreneurs, we are our own leaders.

## Chief Enthusiasm Inspirer

If a business is to succeed and prosper, its purpose must inspire *enthusiasm* in others. As an entrepreneur, you need to inspire enthusiasm so effectively that people are willing to risk money to fund your venture, to forgo other opportunities in order to work for you, and to vote with their wallets by paying money to buy what you offer.

Seeing enthusiasm in others is what tells you that there's a market for what you are doing. If you have a purpose that inspires enthusiasm, then all other problems are mere details. If your purpose doesn't inspire enthusiasm, every little detail will become an insurmountable problem.

As a business founder, you will be *the prime source* of enthusiasm for the venture. It is your responsibility to ensure that the venture itself is doing something that inspires enthusiasm in its customers, its staff and its stakeholders. Your role is to make sure that the purpose is evident in everything that the business does, and in all the decisions you make. If you become an entrepreneur, your real job title is Chief Enthusiasm Inspirer.

When you start a business, the only thing that you really have to sell is your enthusiasm. All that you have is the belief in your purpose, the conviction that you can make it work, and optimism about your prospects. This "can do" attitude is vital, especially given just how little else there is in the beginning. In other words, you need to be a leader for yourself. A leader keeps the business "on purpose" and serves as the ultimate source of enthusiasm for it.

## Your Business Is Not About You

As an entrepreneur, you need to focus on what will inspire others because ultimately your business is not about you. If your only motivation to start a business is to provide yourself with a source of passive income, I believe you will find it very hard to inspire others. I'm all for making a fortune, but the desire to make oneself rich is not an inspiring goal for anybody else. It's not a cause for which other people will storm the barricades.

You will only inspire enthusiasm if you can define a purpose for your business that other people can understand and support. If your business has a meaningful reason for existing, then you will capture people's emotional commitment to it. How are you going to make other people's lives better? For the business to work, you need to make sure it's going to deliver something that other people will want.

It may seem counterintuitive, but when you put aside your ego and concentrate on a higher goal for your business, you end up with more confidence in yourself. When you really care about the purpose of your business, you become an unselfconscious agent of that purpose, focused on seeing it through. The more time I spent thinking about what my business needed in order to succeed, the less time I wasted worrying about whether or not *I* was "a success." That made me more proactive and more confident in myself.

Find something that you believe in; by doing so, you will strengthen your belief in yourself.

## A Purpose That You Care About

Being an entrepreneur means that you get to decide what to work on, so there's no better opportunity to choose a purpose that you really care about. This is one of the great benefits of starting a business. You only get to do your best work in life if you work on something that is truly meaningful to you.

It is horribly depressing to work on something that you don't care about. How many thousands of times do you tell others about what you do for a living? Each of those conversations with customers, colleagues, friends, and family is either an opportunity to talk about the most meaningful purpose that you can imagine, or talk about how you spend so much of your precious time on something that doesn't matter to you.

Only if you believe in the purpose of your business yourself will you inspire enthusiasm in others. Entrepreneurs have to be able to talk convincingly about their ventures, even in the face of setbacks that sometimes feel exhausting and demoralizing. If you believe in your business, selling to customers is simply the fulfillment of your purpose. You are not going to have confidence in selling a mediocre product that doesn't really make anyone's life better. This will be obvious to customers. However, if you are genuinely enthusiastic about your business and you believe in the value of your product, customers will sense your authenticity and they will believe in your product too.

The purpose of your business has to be something that gets you out of bed in the morning when the going gets tough. If you're going to do all this hard work, it has to be on something that you feel is worth doing with your life. Ask yourself if you find it meaningful enough to give you stamina through the inevitable setbacks. As Nietzsche said, "Give a man a *why,* and he can bear almost any *how.*"

If you are doing something truly fulfilling—something you believe in for its own sake—then you get fulfillment every day in the act of doing it, regardless of your financial endgame. If you find purpose in your work that is so important to you that nobody can rob you of your own enthusiasm in pursuit of it, you cannot lose. Your time will be well spent, whatever the outcome, because you will be working on something that *you* value.

## How to Choose a Purpose

If you find it hard to identify an inspiring purpose for your business, you might be making it harder for yourself than it needs to be. Your purpose does not have to be so lofty that you can never realistically pursue it. Many people would like to start a business, but they have adopted unattainable standards for themselves regarding the great deeds that they would have to perform with their venture. They might get deep satisfaction from their ability to deliver value in some area, but if they see nothing obviously "worthy" in what they are good at, then they can't get excited about making it a business.

In this way of thinking, it's somehow OK just to work an office job if you are working for someone else, but if you were to be an entrepreneur yourself then your company would have to be saving the world. What pressure! It's no wonder some people find it hard to get started in business. The idea of taking responsibility for their own venture has become a moral challenge.

Perhaps you have built up the idea in your mind that your very best work, your life's work, would be something that all would recognize instantly as commendable. In this way of thinking, starting a business is only a worthwhile pursuit if it does something that is obviously a great betterment to humanity. You might be concerned that if you go into business without this great sense of purpose, you will only get caught up in a superficial motivation to make money.

This is where your ethics come into the picture. To my mind, the key to becoming a successful entrepreneur on a personal level is to live according to your ethical code. Although your business might not change the world in the grandest way, you will make a change. And perhaps most importantly, creating and running your business will change *you* for the better. You will spend every day helping others and building positive, reciprocal relationships. Through this, you will learn the valuable lessons necessary for growing a business someday that truly reflects your life's deepest calling.

If you create genuine, ethical relationships with your customers, you will have a positive impact on the world, even if your business's core purpose is not grandiose. Some people call themselves "social entrepreneurs" in order to emphasize that their focus is "not just on profit, but on solving a social problem."[5] But the fact is that all entrepreneurs who act with basic ethics solve social problems—in fact, that's what entrepreneurship is all about.

What is a social problem anyway? It's just a living condition that people wish to change. It could be anything that makes people unhappy in their lives. Solving a social problem, therefore, means changing people's conditions, giving them more resources and options. That's exactly what all entrepreneurs do. In this sense, the people who created the first refrigerators were "social entrepreneurs," as were the people who created the first personal computers. On a more basic level, the person who made the first pizza delivery service available in your neighborhood was a social entrepreneur, too.

We need resources to solve any social problem, but resources are scarce. Scarcity is the most fundamental social problem of all. It's the unifying *mega-problem*: our limited resources. Any particular limited resource (time, technology, energy) is interrelated to all the other limited resources. All social problems are subsets of this scarcity problem. If we had unlimited resources, we'd have no social problems. The extent to which we can increase our resources is the extent to which we can solve anything.

Therefore, anyone interested in solving social problems must look at how we can generate additional resources and make them available to society. Although many people assume that things will always just somehow keep getting better, resources don't increase by themselves. If you want to help humanity, you can't take increasing wealth and development for granted. The only way to truly solve social problems is to generate additional resources. As long as you act with basic ethics, then your actions as an entrepreneur will help to make the world better, even if you are "only" creating a local pizza delivery business.

There is no need to agonize over how you can do good in the world. All you need to do is go out there and generate value that makes customers happy. If you can do that without being unethical, you've contributed to chipping away at the biggest, baddest mega-problem that humanity faces. You can free up some resources in the world by making your customers' lives a little easier or more enjoyable. You'll make them more productive and, in their turn, they will have more chance to do their bit to work on generating more resources for humanity. That is how the world gets better.

## Expressing Your Purpose

A vital skill for every entrepreneur is the ability to explain one's purpose in a way that is easy to understand. Nobody is going to be enthusiastic about your offering if it is not clear what your business is all about.

You need an "elevator pitch" for your business if you want to inspire people with your purpose. An elevator pitch is a summary that is so concise, you could explain it to anyone who happens to travel in an elevator with you. If you only had the time it takes to travel a few floors, how could you summarise your startup's purpose?

Expressing your purpose might take some time and might evolve as your business evolves. It's not easy, as it's far outside the employee mentality in which we've been trained. Most entrepreneurs have an intuition about it without being able to express the vision clearly.

David Allen, the productivity expert and creator of the "Getting Things Done"[6] method, observed this about purpose in businesses:

> I've yet to come across a new organization that was confident enough that it could express, in full awareness, its mission and purpose and could state it clearly any sooner than five years from its beginnings. The purpose is certainly there from the start in the form of the fire in the belly of the founders who have the commitment to bring it to life, but to express it in a tangible, conscious, and intellectually definable form is usually a long-term process requiring a depth of experience and seasoned intention to understand and expand the DNA of what drives the enterprise.[7]

Don't get stressed about not being able to clearly express your purpose in the very beginning of your business. You may need to become conscious of it by the doing of the business itself: the very experience of getting your business going clarifies your purpose.

There are some techniques that you can use to help clarify and express your purpose. The traditional way of expressing a company's purpose is as part of the "mission statement." Stephen Covey popularized the idea of the mission statement in his book *The Seven Habits of Highly Effective People*[8] as a way to clarify the purpose of an organization by writing it down. Although the intention is good, mission statements themselves are often wordy and uninspiring. They often try to say so much that they end up being too long to effectively communicate anything at all.

If making a mission statement totally clarifies your core purpose, good for you. As an alternative, you can try Guy Kawasaki's idea of creating a "mantra."[9] A mantra defines your business in literally three words. As an example, he suggests that the owners of Wendy's (the US restaurant chain) should replace their corporate-speak mission statement with three words that clarify their purpose: "healthy fast food." That's the kind of simplicity that you need in order to explain your purpose in an inspiring way.

I found it very hard to get down to such a condensed explanation of what my business stood for. We had struggled with wordy explanations for years before we were finally able to explain simply that we provided "pedestrian movement consulting." That really worked because it made it sound like what we did was part of a well-established field, even though there was no such thing at the time.

## Making the World a Better Place

When people think about making the world better, they usually think first about politics. That's what I learned about in school: a long list of rulers, politicians, and political activists who did great deeds. But politics isn't the way the world gets better, and activists are not the real revolutionaries.

The real revolutionaries are the entrepreneurs. All economic and social progress comes from entrepreneurship. It was entrepreneurs who created the advanced environments that we live in and the amazing products that we use. Indeed, entrepreneurs are ultimately responsible for the social changes that have resulted from all the opportunities that these developments have given us. Thanks to entrepreneurs, we have the privilege to live in a time when most of us don't fear starvation, as the majority of people did for almost all of human history.

Here's how to identify a business purpose that truly inspires enthusiasm: do something that improves the lives of others and thereby makes the world a better place. It doesn't have to be massive. You don't have to aspire to be Richard Branson,[10] who started his first business when he was still in school, and by the age of twenty-two had founded the company that became the Virgin Group (now comprising over four hundred businesses). My company was tiny—it wouldn't even show up on the radar when compared to companies that you have heard of. But it was doing something that helped others, which I strongly believed in. That's all any entrepreneur needs.

Your business purpose doesn't have to involve the alleviation of obvious and direct misery because every effort to make life easier and increase resources helps every other effort to do so. Solving social problems is a global team effort undertaken by everyone who runs a business ethically.

You can always find something to do that you think will improve other people's lives in some way. When was the last time you felt frustrated at how something was done? I was annoyed most times I wanted to cross the street as a pedestrian; I encountered massively inconvenient crossings with buttons that I had to press in order to ask permission to walk. What makes you feel outraged? If you put your mind to it, every day you will notice a senseless waste of human effort in the way that people have to do things now. It doesn't have to be a new product or service. You might see an opportunity to reimagine an existing service by making it cheaper, or by creating a friendlier customer experience.

Choose a goal that makes you feel excited about the possibilities of joy, pleasure, and love that you could unleash through a new way of doing things. So much is going to change about your business once you get it going that you need something underneath that you can truly believe in.

When you are working on something that you think is worthwhile, it will get you out of bed in the morning. The fear of failure that every entrepreneur experiences doesn't go away, but if you really believe in what you are doing because it brings more happiness to other people, and thereby improves the world (however specific and small that improvement is), then you'll feel the fear and do it anyway.

If you do become an entrepreneur, you will be one of the real revolutionaries. If you do it right, you will change the world.

Here are the three most important things to remember about finding purpose in business:

- Your job as an entrepreneur is to be Chief Enthusiasm Inspirer for a purpose that others can rally to.
- If you choose a purpose for your business that you

genuinely care about, it will keep you going during the hard times.
- Find a way to express your purpose as simply as possible, ideally in three words.

CHAPTER FOUR

# Learn by Selling

*I have never worked a day in my life without selling. If I believe in something, I sell it, and I sell it hard.*

—Estée Lauder

Selling is the aspect of entrepreneurship that most strongly contradicts our conditioning. We've been trained to believe that we are not supposed to speak about our positive qualities. We've also been taught that we are not supposed to talk plainly about money. Yet in order to sell, you have to present the positive qualities of something that you have made and ask directly for money. I found this very uncomfortable at first.

I felt vulnerable when I started to sell. I had to be up front about why I thought that hiring my business would be the best choice for potential clients. I knew I was opening myself up to criticism by directly expressing my enthusiasm and positivity about the business. I found that scary.

I also felt vulnerable about asking to get paid in return for our services. I worried that new contacts would dislike me for bringing money into the relationship. I worried that

I would make a fool of myself, especially if I misjudged the pricing. Most of all, I worried about being rejected, since selling involves so much rejection.

I avoided selling, in order to avoid the discomfort that it provoked in me. I could always find seemingly useful things to do instead. You may also find it very uncomfortable to get out there and sell if it directly contradicts deep-seated messages that you have learned. Many people prefer the comfort of being an employee and getting a paycheck just so they don't have to face the psychological challenge of selling. Selling makes everyone feel vulnerable, but it gets easier the more you do it.

In this chapter, I will highlight some of the most prevalent conditioning against selling and suggest ways to overcome it. I will explain why selling is so important to your business because it is how you learn what works as an entrepreneur.

## Principled and Unprincipled Selling

Every culture has prejudices about selling. The worst prejudice is the idea that selling is all about bullying and manipulation. Mainstream movies and novels portray salespeople as pushy and unprincipled.

The unspoken assumption behind this cultural prejudice is that *all* salespeople are unprincipled. Of course, this is not true. There are principled salespeople and unprincipled salespeople. When salespeople act in an unprincipled way, they are no longer selling; they are doing something else, such as defrauding. For example, there are salespeople who lie about the benefits of a product in an attempt to persuade you to buy it. I would call that fraud, not selling.

It is also true that some salespeople use manipulative tactics to try to close a sale. However, that behavior is not inherent in selling. Some people try to use psychological manipulation to get dates, but that doesn't mean that dating itself is about manipulation. The same applies to selling.

Principled selling is rooted in principled negotiation. Negotiation does not have to be a battle of wills: it can be a collaborative search for win-win outcomes using objective means. Principled negotiation is a fundamental skill for entrepreneurs that most parents don't teach their kids, and that most schools and universities ignore. I didn't even know there was a body of knowledge about negotiation from which I could learn.

*Getting to Yes*[11] by Fisher and Ury is widely considered the best book on negotiation; it's certainly the best thing that I've read on the topic. It provides a systematic and principled approach to negotiating win-win outcomes. I adopted Fisher and Ury's approach completely, which made both my negotiation and my selling far more effective.

Principled selling is simply persuasion. Nobody has to buy anything from a seller; the seller has to convince the buyer of the benefits. If a buyer parts with their money, it's because they value whatever benefits they receive more highly than the money they give away. By definition, a sale is always voluntary, so there is nothing morally wrong with it.

## Overcoming Ignorance About Selling

I was ignorant about selling when I started my business. I had not taken an active sales role in previous jobs, so I had very little sales experience. In school and college I learned nothing whatsoever about selling, despite the fact that it is a crucial life skill. Teachers are insulated from the need to sell. Consequently, they are generally ignorant about selling and tend to be prejudiced against it.

Selling was the last thing that I thought about or wanted to do. My interest lay in developing the technology of our product. I know many people who had a similar experience. When you get going, you want to create your awesome new gadget or service. It's fun and interesting: you're doing something new. It's not stressful, because it's entirely under your control. But actually, those activities are often a convenient distraction from what you really need to be doing, which is selling.

As soon as you become an entrepreneur, you're in the selling business. Entrepreneurship is all about getting agreements and persuading people of the benefits of a particular action. The action might be to buy your product, use your service, give you a referral, fund your business, come and work for you, or set up an affiliate link with you. All of these agreements are dependent on your selling skills. It's important to learn to find satisfaction and fulfillment through selling as quickly as possible because if there's no selling, then there's no business, and you'll have to pack up and go home.

When I came to understand selling in a systematic way, it enabled me to identify the right activities that I could do to help improve the sales process and shape my business. That felt great and gave me a real sense of satisfaction.

Selling is something that you can break down and understand as a process of stages, each with its own measurable characteristics. I encourage you to read everything that you can about selling and get beyond the amateur phase as quickly as you can. I personally found it helpful to read the most unapologetic and assertive books on selling that I could find, the most useful of which for me was *How to Master the Art of Selling* by Tom Hopkins.[12]

## Selling Is a Numbers Game

In the beginning, selling can seem like a painful process of repeated rejection. It can be frustrating when you face a lot of indifference. Increasing sales can be a slow process. Everybody is busy. Customers don't think that they require what you are selling. They may not immediately react to your great offering with anything like the enthusiasm that you hope for. I avoided focusing on selling at first because receiving these kinds of responses made me feel uncomfortable.

However, when you start to get a handle on it, you realize that selling is just a numbers game. It is true that when you try to make sales, many people will turn your offer down. However, as long as you approach the process strategically, every sales attempt will give you useful information. By adjusting both your offering and your sales approach in light of each new bit of information, you get better and better at improving your success ratio.

Selling teaches you resilience because, as with everything in business, you experience so much failure. Attempting sales and failing teaches you to keep trying. You learn to focus on the results as a whole, not the outcome of an individual sale.

When you accept that it's a numbers game, rejection becomes less significant and you don't take it personally, because you realize that it doesn't matter if a particular customer doesn't buy. It's just part of the process; other customers will buy. If you qualify your sales prospects and identify benefits for customers, then selling becomes more about building relationships.

## Selling Is About Nurturing Relationships

Many people think that in order to sell, you have to be brash and pushy. Selling does teach you assertiveness, but it also teaches you humility. It teaches you not to feel entitled to anyone else's time, attention, or money. It teaches you the value of empathy and reciprocity.

As with all relationships, you need to empathize with your customers if you want to nurture your relationships with them. Empathy comes from working to understand their needs, so that you can identify ways to provide value to them. There's no guarantee that customers will be interested in the value that you believe you can provide.

Nurturing your relationships with customers is vital to

the growth of your business because the majority of your sales are likely to come in the form of repeat business from those existing customers. Existing customers are the engine of your growth. You also get *referrals* from them, whereby existing customers "refer" new customers to your product or service by recommending it to them. I wasn't familiar with this concept when I started my business, but it's one of the most important ways to grow sales.

Partner and affiliate relationships are also amazing drivers of growth. Partnering involves identifying other people who sell a complementary product and linking with them to provide a joint offering that is even more beneficial to the customer than either product by itself. Alternatively, you can sometimes piggyback on a partner's sales process by adding your product or service to what they are already selling.

For example, I developed a partnering scheme to link up with architectural firms. Our clients were retail development companies who bought pedestrian movement consulting from us because they wanted to ensure that their new shopping malls would have good shopper flows on all levels. We realized that architects could use our services on the retail projects that they were designing. Although the developers paid our bills, the architects were the ones who helped us get the sale.

Most of the time, selling is about looking after relationships. Consequently, any fears that you may have about selling may not even be appropriate to the reality of what you'll end up doing. It really pays off to get into selling right away. It's not only super important; it's also incredibly interesting and rewarding, and a huge amount of personal growth is involved. You will learn both about yourself and about negotiation. Selling may be scary, but the fear signifies a massive potential for personal growth.

## Creating Your Own Opportunities

I started out thinking I would sell when an obvious opportunity arose. However, selling opportunities very rarely arise on their own. They don't happen unless you dedicate the time to creating them. To succeed, I had to set aside significant chunks of time to focus exclusively on new business generation. I blocked out my calendar every Tuesday and devoting that day entirely to generating new sales leads. That worked for me as I could get into the mindset and just sell all day. I would follow up and respond to e-mails during the rest of the week, but I devoted one entire day each week to generating new business.

It was easier for me to get in the zone for a day, but other people find it helpful to spend a couple of hours selling every morning. They don't look at e-mails; they close the door and make themselves otherwise unavailable. Whatever time you prefer, I suggest you devote a bare minimum of one and a half hours a day or one day a week solely to new business generation.

However, dedicating time and resources to selling is only going to help if your selling is effective. In order to be successful, you need systems to track which sales efforts are working and which are not. This information, or *business intelligence*, allows you to course-correct and improve your sales. How to acquire this information is the subject of the next chapter.

The necessity of selling is difficult but also wonderfully purifying for your business. It casts out self-preoccupations and ensures that your venture does things that are truly valuable to others. In this way, it brings you closer to fulfilling your own potential. Believe it or not, when you come to see selling in this way, it becomes fun.

## Selling Shapes Your Business

Selling is of paramount importance not simply because it is how you get money into your business (although the revenue is vital too, of course). The real value of selling is that it is a learning mechanism. The best guide to whether your business is on track is whether your customers will pay for your product or service. Payment from your customers does not have to be only in the form of money: it could also be in the form of referrals, recommendations, or useful feedback about your product. The key is that your customers signal their recognition and appreciation, through some form of reciprocation That means paying you for your product or service.

Payment is the feedback that you need in order to course-correct and guide you in your business. Payment from a customer is like a message that says, "What you do improves my life, so I am willing to show my appreciation by giving something back." This is the most useful information anyone can give you about where to take your business.

For this reason, it's vital to start selling as quickly as possible. You probably want to improve your product, develop your marketing materials, and do any number of other important things before you start selling. However, the sooner you sell something to somebody, the sooner you will actually learn whether or not your offering improves the lives of your customers and how it could do so more effectively. This is also how you learn what you might need to change about your business in order to better help your customers.

Many entrepreneurs emphasize the importance of beginning to sell as soon as possible. The central idea of the *Lean Startup*[13] movement is to treat your business development as a process of validated learning about which product developments work. Selling is the vehicle for this learning, and your validation comes in the way that your customers respond to your sales attempts. The idea is to develop a "minimum viable product," which is the simplest version of your offer that you can get to market as quickly as possible.

You race to selling because it provides the best feasibility test of any business idea. Reid Hoffman, the founder of LinkedIn, suggests that entrepreneurs should focus all their efforts on getting to the first potential failure point as quickly as possible, so that they can test the viability of their venture before putting more effort into it.[14] This is the pass-or-fail point: Can you make something that will actually sell?

Selling fundamentally shaped my business. When I started Intelligent Space, I wanted to develop an application service provision business model (ASP), whereby we would provide online software that our clients could use for a specialist type of computer simulation. This system would have been very expensive to develop and would have taken a lot of time to implement. We began by selling consulting services with the aim of financing the development of our application service from revenue.

Once we started selling to customers, we soon learned that they did not want an application service. Our clients wanted us to help them get better results as architects, engineers, and shopping center developers. They didn't want us to help them become pedestrian movement experts. They wanted *us* to take responsibility for telling them how well their design would work for pedestrian flow, and how they could make it better.

Our clients made it clear, through what they were willing to pay for, that they wanted an answer handed to them. They wanted that answer in a form that was easy to understand, such as an animation of pedestrians walking around their shopping mall. They also wanted someone there in important meetings with them to tackle any difficult questions about the pedestrian model. In short, they wanted us to do consultancy work, which is not what I originally wanted to do.

That was how the process of selling influenced the evolution of our business model. We changed the goal for our business model two years after founding. We dropped our plans to sell software and deliberately focused on developing a consultancy service. In this way, we allowed ourselves to be influenced by what our customers were willing to pay for.

Here are the most important points to remember about selling:

- The main value of selling is that it is a learning process. It shapes your business by providing you with essential feedback about what works.
- Every entrepreneur needs this learning process in order to succeed, so it's vital to start selling as soon as possible and devote significant time to it on an ongoing basis.
- Ignorance and prejudice surround the act of selling, but the reality is that principled selling is a mutually beneficial activity that nurtures relationships.

Entrepreneurship is fundamentally a process of experimental learning through selling. The market is an evolutionary process that develops by trial and error, with businesses starting, experimenting, evolving, and changing. In the same way, your business will be a trial and error machine. You can't know in advance what you might offer that will really evoke enthusiasm in your customers, but you can make judgment calls and you can *experiment*. To be effective, any experiment requires feedback from your customers. The best way to get feedback is to try to sell.

CHAPTER FIVE

# The Unexamined Business Is Not Worth Building

*The unexamined life is not worth living.*
—Socrates

There is always so much to do in any new business. You could easily work ten hours every day of the week and still feel as though you had more to do. I felt that way most of the time in the first years, as do many entrepreneurs. I ran from one emergency to the next. I lacked a strategic way of working. I didn't feel like I had control.

You need to understand your business in order to control it. As an employee, you don't get a chance to acquire a strategic overview of the company you work for, so there is much less opportunity to understand how it works. You don't get to think about the big picture much because you do not run the business—the business runs you. In contrast, when you start your own business, you *can* get the most comprehensive overview of the operation possible.

However, this overview does not happen automatically. You need to be proactive about tracking and analyzing your business in order to understand exactly what is going on. Without a proactive approach to mapping out your business, you will be just as unaware of the big picture as most employees are. Events will constantly surprise you, and you will probably spend much of your time firefighting—as I did before I started tracking consistently.

This proactive approach to tracking and analyzing a business is very different from what we are all accustomed to. Our employee conditioning trains us all to expect somebody else to tell us how we are doing and what is happening. However, as a business owner, nobody else is there to tell you how you or the business are doing. It's up to you to work that out for yourself.

Breaking the employee paradigm involves measuring everything important about your business, including your own activity, and then doing something worthwhile with the information. This means collecting objective data about how your business is doing, and adjusting your operations continually, in light of this data.

This chapter is a little more technical than previous ones, as it includes concrete examples of proactive tracking and analysis. Although the specific techniques and measures that I describe are useful in and of themselves, the real reason I've gone into such detail is to give you a realistic sense of what it is like to adopt this approach. When I started to track and analyze my business consistently, I truly understood how it worked and, most importantly, I understood what wasn't working. This freed me from a lot of stress and significantly improved my decisions. If you adopt this approach, it will free you too.

## Planning Versus Tracking

Planning your business can be a waste of time if you don't have a framework in place for tracking it. When I started my business, I had a clear idea of where I wanted to go and what I wanted to do. My business partner and I wrote a detailed business plan with many graphs and charts showing projected performance: how big our sales were going to be, how many people we would employ, etc. Once we got going, however, that original business plan went out of the window.

As I described in chapter four, we initially intended to develop a web-based application to support architects and developers, but we ended up creating a consultancy because that is what our customers wanted. The business *opportunity* led us to consulting, despite the fact that this was not our original business *plan*.

The goals within your business plan express what you want to happen, which can be very different from what actually happens. Jason Fried and David Heinemeier Hannsson are the founders of 37Signals.com—a company that provides web-based collaboration tools. They suggest that business plans should be called *business guesses*[15] because that's exactly what they are. Something as fundamental as your business model may change from what you anticipated in your original business plan.

A business plan is useful, even though it's full of guesses. It is a good place to capture your purpose, by writing down your mission statement or mantra (as discussed in chapter three). Writing your purpose down and revising it as needed is important: the act of writing helps to increase your awareness of the reasons you are doing this in the first place.

Your business plan is also useful as a written summary of how your business will work financially. This means writing down in simple terms how you propose to take in more money than you spend while pursuing your purpose. If you can explain this in simple terms, you have a useful business plan. If you don't have a clear story as to how you propose to earn more money than you spend, then you have a problem.

It may also be helpful to outline simple, measurable goals that you think are the most relevant to the fulfillment of your purpose, along with the steps you plan to take in order to reach them. Derek Sivers, founder of cdbaby.com, has this advice: "A business plan should never take more than a few hours of work. Hopefully no more than a few minutes. The best plans start simple. A quick glance and common sense should tell you if the numbers will work. The rest are details."[16]

There's nothing wrong with writing short, easily understandable business plans; it's really helpful to clarify your vision and your purpose for the business. However, many entrepreneurs focus on the planning side of their business and put surprisingly little effort into tracking the reality of what is actually going on in their business. Your business plan is your intended strategy, but the way that you allocate your time and resources is your actual, emergent strategy.

## The Value of Tracking

Whereas the importance of projections and goals in business plans can be overrated, business tracking and analysis is absolutely vital. The most valuable asset that you have is your business intelligence. This includes things like your list of business contacts, information you gather about potential sales, your analysis of profitability on each project, and your web analytics. This information is golden. If I wanted to buy your business, I would be more interested in this data than in anything you wrote in your business plan.

When you get going, reality will not unfold according to your plans. So how do you best adjust and course-correct? By tracking reality and by seeing what's actually going on. This gives you the necessary information to make a conscious decision about how to adapt, what to change, and where to direct your business.

That might sound a bit abstract, so this chapter provides some examples of what you can track to improve your business intelligence. We'll apply tracking and analysis to sales as a first example, since selling is such a crucial activity. In later chapters, we will apply tracking and analysis to other aspects of running a business.

The more you can track what you're doing, the more you're able to be conscious about how your business is evolving. That information itself will guide you into making new decisions and course corrections, reallocating your resources and your time in a way that you know will drive the business forward.

Tracking is where your sense of efficacy in business comes from. My level of enjoyment in running a business relates directly to how transparent the business is to me. If I can understand and track what is happening, I can cope with any setback because I know what impact my actions have.

In contrast, if I am not getting any feedback about how effective my actions are, every task seems harder and more stressful. It's no fun running in the dark. We need the feedback that comes from measurement.

Tracking gives you the freedom to experiment. I can try things out if I know I will get useful information by tracking the results, so an experiment is never wasted—even if it doesn't work. If I could never find out whether an experiment worked, why would I put effort into trying it? You need feedback in any trial-and-error process in order to correct the errors.

Building up your business intelligence is about becoming an expert in your venture and all facts related to it. This means building, maintaining and analyzing databases concerning all aspects of your operation. Consider it your job to be an expert in everything to do with your business because that information is the most valuable asset you have.

The relevant information will vary somewhat by industry and individual business. In the rest of this chapter, I'll provide some examples based on what was important for my own business.

## Marketing Data

The most important measurements for marketing are those that show how well each marketing activity is performing relative to its cost to you. You may not be able to tell in advance how successful a particular channel is going to be, but you can always gather information about how well it is performing once it is underway. This information allows you to course-correct and focus your efforts on the most useful channels.

There are many ways to track the value of specific marketing activities that you do, but the underlying principle is the same for all of them: gather data on the level of response to each campaign or channel. For example, for each marketing campaign, you can use different web links (with a service like bitly.com) and different Voice-over-IP phone numbers to identify which campaign brought in each response. You can use different e-mails for different campaigns (e.g., one e-mail for your business card, another for your website, and another for an affiliate program).

You can easily capture a huge amount of useful information about activity on your website. There are plenty of resources online that explain how to collect and analyze these kinds of data. The goal is to identify what ultimately leads to sales. For example, is there a difference in the conversion rate (number of purchases per view) between specific product pages, and if so, why?

You may participate in industry events like conferences and trade fairs, especially if your company sells business to business. Tracking your participation in events like these will help you understand objectively whether or not you need to get more serious about putting yourself out there and getting yourself known to potential customers and clients, or whether the activities that you have been doing in this respect are a waste of time. I used a database to track many aspects of my participation in industry events, such as the number of events I participated in each month and the number of presentations I made.

You can also treat each industry event as a marketing channel in your analysis, tracking responses to the material you present or hand out at each event, so that you can see what level of response each event brings. I tracked the number of new contacts I met at each event and the number of projects arising from those contacts. These kinds of measurements identify what you are doing proactively to increase your relationships within your industry, and whether your actions are worthwhile.

## Sales Data

Being conscious about selling involves tracking your sales pipeline: your opportunities or potential sales. Building a database containing potential revenue-generating opportunities is extremely valuable; it is literally a database containing sources of money that you could either earn or miss! If you have a web-only business, this might be your e-mail subscriber list. For a consultancy firm, you could build a database of potential projects from your contact with clients.

Sometimes there are important bits of information that you might like to capture but cannot get exact numbers for. In such cases, if you have enough information to make an informed guess, then it is very much worth capturing your estimate. For example, we estimated the likely fee and guessed the probability of each potential consulting project happening, even though the estimates changed during negotiation. Our running estimates enabled us to calculate a probability-adjusted fee for every potential project, even the early opportunities. We also estimated the likeliest start date, so that we could estimate when revenue would be coming in and thereby inform our cash flow planning.

One of the most useful bits of information to capture about potential sales is the origin of each selling opportunity. This shows how your customers are coming to you. For example, we tracked whether consulting projects were initiated by clients, follow-ups from a previous project, generated from an affiliate or partner, the result of active sales activity, or referrals. This data taught us the value of looking after our existing customers, as referrals and repeat business soon became the majority of our work.

We also analyzed the origin of each sales opportunity by its business sector (for example, retail or transport). This allowed us to look at which sectors generated more work over time and whether our success rate differed for project proposals in each sector. This kind of information helped target our selling activity on those areas where we were most likely to succeed.

## People Data

Your list of contacts is probably the most valuable resource in your business. Business opportunities don't just float in the clouds; they are always attached to a person. It's not only customers that matter; other vital business relationships include partners, affiliates, referral sources, suppliers, and so on. The information about people acts as a link between all your other business databases.[17]

Information about business contacts can be stored in a simple address book. However, if you want to undertake useful analysis and tracking, you will need to implement a more flexible database, such as a customer relationship management (CRM) system. There are plenty of existing CRM tools that you can use, or you can build your own database (which is what we did).

You can analyze a huge amount of useful information regarding contacts. For example, we tracked the number of sales from each customer, the number of referrals from each person, and the number of projects we collaborated on with each industry partner.

In this way, we built up a picture of who was behind the growth of our business. We knew who was connecting us to potential sales, who brought the most work to us in the previous year and who gave us the most profitable projects. This allowed us to ensure that we devoted attention to the people who really deserved it.

You can also track your own activity related to meeting people, in order to understand the effect of your own actions on the development of your business network. I tracked the number of potential new customers, partners, and affiliates that I met per month as well as the number of face-to-face meetings I had within each category of contact.

These are all measurements related to your connection with other people, and the activities or business consequences that arise from them. This information helps you decide which relationships you need to spend more time developing, and which ones are not bringing value. In this way, you can focus your time more productively.

## Socrates Was Right

Here are the most important points to remember about planning and tracking:

- A business plan can be a useful way to summarize your business's purpose, the means by which you propose to make money, and the steps that you intend to take in order to reach a few easily understandable goals. Nonetheless, your business plan is just a guess that will change over time.
- Business tracking is more valuable than planning. It is the most important guide for all your activities. The information (or business intelligence) collected by tracking is the most valuable asset you have.
- In order to gather business intelligence, you need to build, maintain, and analyze databases concerning all aspects of your operation. This chapter has

provided examples of data collection relating to marketing and sales activities.

The examples in this chapter are not meant to be an exhaustive list; you can track a lot of other relevant sales metrics for your particular industry. In chapter six, we'll look at how to apply this approach to finance. In chapter eight, we'll apply it to profitability.

The point of all this tracking is to be conscious of what you are doing. Your emergent strategy (what you are *really* doing) trumps your planned strategy (what you *think* you are doing). As Socrates said, "The unexamined life is not worth living." Equally, the unexamined business is not worth building.

CHAPTER SIX

# The Best Funding There Is

*Watch out when anyone (including you) says he wants to do something big, but can't until he raises money. It usually means the person is more in love with the idea of being big big big than with actually doing something useful. For an idea to get big big big, it has to be useful. And being useful doesn't need funding.*

—Derek Sivers

I was ignorant about finance when I started my business. The fact that I have always been relatively frugal gave me an advantage, as I had some savings that I could use to fund the startup period. However, I still depleted all my reserves, took on debts, and spent more than I needed to in order to get the business going. Over time, I came to understand a much better way to fund a business.

Employee conditioning provides no preparation for the challenges of raising capital in business. When you are an employee, someone else created your job for you. You work in a building leased or bought by someone else, using resources obtained for you by someone else. How did it all get there? As an employee, that's not your concern.

In contrast, if you do want to start a business, you have

this completely unfamiliar challenge of how to finance it. Nothing in your employee life prepares you for how to tackle financing questions. Yet every entrepreneur faces the same question at the beginning: How do you finance the initial period of developing your capability, before you start making big sales?

The way that you choose to tackle this question can have a huge impact on the level of autonomy that you experience as an entrepreneur. On one hand, you lack resources in the beginning, and you need resources in order to create a new business. On the other hand, the more funding you take from other people, the less autonomy you have—thereby removing one of the most appealing aspects of starting a business.

My short answer to the funding question for the vast majority of startups is this: the best way to finance your business is through your own money—incrementally through sales income from the business itself, supplemented at the start by your own savings, if necessary. Funding yourself is better for your business focus, your autonomy as an entrepreneur, and your ultimate financial freedom. In this chapter I will explain how to fund yourself, and why I think it is the best way to go. We'll also review the other options open to you and look at how they compare.

## Bootstrapping

Bootstrapping is the ultimate solution for any entrepreneur who wants to preserve their freedom. The term bootstrapping comes from the idea of pulling yourself up by your own bootstraps. In other words, you are financing your own growth. If you do finance yourself, then you do not have to sell partial ownership of your business, you do not have to pay back loans, and you do not have to deal with all of the complications involved in getting finance from other people. If you can bootstrap yourself, you maintain maximum control.

There are two ways of bootstrapping. First, you can finance yourself through your own savings. If you have some money saved when you start your business, then you can draw on that money to finance the initial period before you start bringing in revenue. The more savings you have, the longer you will have before you go into debt.

There's no better way to ensure that you are working on something that you really believe in than to ask yourself if you are willing to use your own savings and risk your own earning capacity in pursuing it.

You are asking everyone, yourself included, to vote with their wallets about whether your project is really worth it. Is your idea important enough that you are willing to put your own money into it? If not, then it's probably not your life's work. Also, you can be pretty sure that nobody else is going to fund your venture if you don't even demonstrate that you are willing to do so yourself, as far as you are able.

I funded my business with my own savings at first. I had some savings that I had accumulated in my twenties, and so did my business partner. We both put money into the business to get things moving. It was not enough for us to get into positive cash flow (I will explain more about other things that we did below), but it enabled us to start developing our services.

Bootstrapping with your own savings is a great thing to do if you can. Obviously, it's dependent on building up savings, which can take significant time. This is why it is so much harder to start an entrepreneurial venture if you already have outstanding debt.

The sooner in life that you start a business the better because the older you get the more commitments you will have (especially if you want to have children). It is definitely going to make the startup period easier if you do it before you have other significant financial responsibilities. That will help you reduce your need for financing and give you a much easier start to the business. I had no debt, no major financial commitments (no kids or mortgage), and some savings.

## Revenue Financing

The other way to bootstrap is to finance the growth of your business through revenue yourself. This is essentially the "do not spend any money until you have it" plan. It is difficult to do because there are always great arguments as to why you need to spend money in the beginning. Whatever business you start, you will probably focus on the things that you need to put in place in order to be credible. Perhaps you will spend money making an amazing website, or perhaps developing technology. All such things cost money.

The idea behind revenue-based self financing is to fund the initial period—before you can make big sales with your full product—by making little sales with your minimum viable product. Every business that will be useful in the long term has value of some kind to offer customers in the beginning.

If you can start selling that value in a simple form as quickly as possible, you can use revenue to finance the growth of the business and develop a more complex offering as you go. Even if you intend to develop a capital-intensive business (for example, one that involves a lot of technology), you might be able to start a capital-light version 1.0 of the business that helps customers in the present, and then incrementally develop a capital-intensive version 2.0 as you go.

Financing yourself through revenue is emotionally challenging. It puts you into that uncomfortable position of going out and selling as quickly as possible with a "minimum viable product." I resisted this approach for the first two years because I was uncomfortable with it. It was much easier to do interesting and "safe" things like develop our website, develop our technology, and focus on other behind-the-scenes stuff that was less emotionally challenging than selling.

## Crowdsourced Revenue Financing

One great kind of revenue financing that has become far easier recently is crowdfunding. This involves an advance sale to a wide group of your customers or fans. In short, you ask customers to support the development of your product by paying money in advance of you actually developing it.

If you raise enough capital, you develop the product and eventually your supporters get their purchased item. Sometimes they don't even get a final product but rather some other reward—perhaps just the good feeling of having helped you get your business off the ground. The model builds on the idea of a subscription-based service, whereby customers pay now to receive a subscription in the future.

Crowdfunding is a brilliant solution to the question of how to finance your startup through revenue. It's great for your cash flow, since you don't have an outlay before having guaranteed customers. It engages you in marketing and selling right at the beginning, enabling you to get valuable feedback from customers before you start spending serious money.

Crowdfunding also carries the advantage of being virtually risk-free with regard to marketing and sales. If your idea gets funded, you start out with an audience of committed buyers; if not, you've just learned without significant expense that your idea still needs work.

There are many services online providing a platform for crowdsourcing, such as Kickstarter[18] and Indiegogo.[19] It's well worth considering a crowdsourced development.

## Why Revenue Financing Is Best

Revenue financing serves as a test of your business strategy. If you can sell a simple version of your product to someone right now, it is a strong indication that you are doing the right thing. If you can't sell anything, then that is valuable information that requires a response. You probably need to adjust your strategy, which is always easier to do early on, before you expend a huge amount of time and effort.

When you pursue revenue financing, you automatically avoid going into more debt than necessary. If you ignore revenue in the initial period and focus on product development, you can spend a lot of money to get your initial product or service ready without knowing anything about whether it will sell. If you are financing through loans, that could mean taking on a lot of debt. However, if you are financing through revenue, you get automatic feedback from the market: no sales means no more spending. Back to the drawing board.

Revenue financing is the best way to enjoy autonomy as an entrepreneur. It allows you to avoid the constraint of being beholden to funders who have their own needs.

If you apply the approach of *doing what people will pay for* to financing, what you get is revenue financing. It keeps you focused on customer needs and on what will sell, which will inform you as to how to invest wisely in your own research and development (R&D). Even though it is difficult, bootstrapping by revenue financing is a brilliant option that I urge you to consider for your own business.

## Loans

There is a huge difference between taking out loans to fund personal consumption (e.g., buying a car or a house) and using a loan to start a value-producing enterprise. Many people are so loaded up with consumption debt that they do not feel able to take the risk of starting a business. Consumption debt limits your opportunities. It is a particularly disempowering aspect of the employee mentality. However, if you use loans to develop an entrepreneurial venture, you are investing in potential future income generation.

The easiest way to take out a loan for your business is to start by asking friends and family, which is what I did. After taking small personal loans from my bank and my father, I approached an entrepreneur friend about financing the startup. Initially, we discussed him taking a share ownership in the business, but we settled on him providing a loan. With interest, it amounted to over £150,000—the equivalent of over $246,000. It took five years to pay it back.

There are other places that you may be able to get loans. You can try to get a bank loan, although it is difficult to borrow much money from banks for startups. There are alternative financing websites that link lenders to small businesses. However, your friends or family members are in a far better position to understand what it is you are doing. You have already earned their trust. They also have a vested interest in wanting to help you.

The fact that I took personal loans was a strong motivator for me to keep going until my business reached profitability; not only because I didn't want to have a large debt hanging over me, but also because I cared about the people who had lent me money. I wanted to make sure that I repaid the trust they showed me.

## Selling Equity

Selling equity in your company is giving part ownership of the business to somebody else in return for financing. An investor provides money to fund the startup and, in return, the entrepreneur gives the investor a share of the ownership of the business. This is the classic entrepreneur's dream that became so popular in the 1990s tech boom: have a cool idea, get venture capital firms to finance it, and thereby avoid the personal risk associated with taking out loans. Many entrepreneurs in that period took the attitude that raising financing was a way to fund their own consumption of other people's money, rather than a way to offer funders a better use for their resources.

This method of financing is very appealing to entrepreneurs because it reduces the amount of risk involved for them. It sounds great, but this is actually a very expensive way of financing your business. A venture capital firm is only going to want to invest in a business if they can make a significant return on their investment because investing in startups is very risky. Consequently, they are going to want perhaps a twentyfold return on investment because one successful investment has to cover all startups they fund that do not give them any return. Understandably, they want enough control and influence to ensure that the company works towards their interests.

You can look at venture capital as a loan combined with an extremely expensive "failure to pay back" insurance policy. When those investors exit, they want to see a far higher return than with a normal loan because they are effectively insuring you against financial risk. You pay for reducing your own risk as an entrepreneur, and you will pay very highly for that.

With venture capital, you also see startups turn into machines for obtaining financing. The entrepreneurs become completely preoccupied with doing presentations to venture capital firms or other potential financing sources, and this becomes the purpose driving their business. It is the opposite of the revenue-financing approach. The pursuit of revenue financing focuses on the needs of your customers; whereas the pursuit of venture capital focuses on making presentations to get funding.

I considered selling equity to the entrepreneur friend that I mentioned above. When I initially approached him, I wanted him to invest in the company. During negotiations, it became clear to me that selling equity would be significantly more expensive than a loan, as he wanted a majority stake in the business. I valued my freedom of action and my control over the business more than I valued the reduced risk. That's why I decided not to sell equity.

Financing comes down to a trade-off between maximizing your freedom and minimizing your financial risk. If you want maximum freedom, then it makes sense to finance the startup through bootstrapping, without selling off any of your business. If you want maximum safety, you can attempt to offload risk onto others and cede part ownership of the venture in return. But owning the business yourself is one of the reasons that you started it in the first place, so there comes a point at which one must ask—why bother being a founder if the business is not really yours?

## The Unexamined Business and Financing

In chapter five, we looked at how tracking your business is more important than planning. This applies to financing too. It's very easy to focus on your intentions for getting money and pay too little attention to the real circumstances of your financial position. If you always stay fully conscious about the financial position of your business by tracking and analyzing your financing data, you will be able to make better decisions about funding.

The most valuable thing that you can do to become conscious about the financial position of your business is this: start tracking *forward cash flow* from day one. You need to know how much money will be coming in and going out each week, as far into the future as possible, taking into account all committed revenue and spending. You can use the forward cash flow tracking feature within your general accounting software to do this, or create your own tool in a spreadsheet.

Whatever tool you use, you will need one that you can show your projected cash flow for the next three to six months (or as far forward as realistically possible), so you know when you're going to pay each bill and when you expect to receive each payment.

You may end up bankrupt if you are not able to anticipate the timing of your cash flow. During the first two years, we had many near emergencies in which we were surprised to find that we had less money than expected. This was usually because we had not anticipated predictable events, such as a client paying their invoice late.

It's easy to look at annual numbers and think you're going to make enough, but your cash flow may get so out of sync with your expenses that you can't make payroll or pay the bills. You need to be able to anticipate shocks to your cash flow, such as a project taking longer than expected or a customer not paying on time. If you are conscious of the status of your cash flow, you are far better able to plan and respond to crises. For this reason, it's crucial to start using a forward cash flow planning tool as soon as you can.

As a business owner, any cash-flow problem affects you personally. I did not pay myself at all for the first year of my business, and only intermittently for the second. After a friend and advisor helped set up our cash flow planning tool, I gained enough control to pay myself regularly.

Cash flow planning is the most valuable activity that you can undertake to increase your awareness about your finances. As a side benefit, you gain all sorts of other useful information in the process, such as who the late payers are. You can rank your customers in terms of their payment reliability, which will let you know about any customers who cause you more problems than they are worth.

## Do You Need Financing?

The final thing to consider about financing is the question of how much money you really need. Entrepreneurs often start with the assumption that they need a lot of financing. I had this assumption: I took out loans to finance the business before I knew how to spend the money wisely. Consequently, in the first year I spent money on stuff that, in hindsight, was not worthwhile.

For example, the entrepreneur friend who lent us the money believed that it was very important for us to have an office, so clients could see that we meant business and we were here to stay. So we got an office, and nobody was remotely interested in visiting us in the first year. Having an office was nice, but we could have significantly reduced our financing needs if we had not rented the premises so quickly.

It's prudent to question how much you actually need financing and to look carefully at what you think you need to spend money on. The temptation is to spend money rather than go out and earn it, because earning via selling is psychologically so much harder. In the early days, we spent a lot of money on things that we could have financed with revenue later. For example, we developed the software that eventually became part of our unique selling proposition; however, none of the revenue that we made in the first year required this software.

Funding makes it very easy to avoid the most uncomfortable actions that you need to take as a business owner. The first year in business exposes your personal weaknesses, and shows what you need to resolve in yourself in order to be effective. For me, this was selling. Without the luxury of funding, however, you know that if you don't do the uncomfortable tasks, then you will go under, so you do them. It may be that I had to run out of money in order to find the resolve to confront my most uncomfortable business tasks. This could be the case for you too. It's better to take less funding and run out of money sooner, rather than later, if that is what helps you change your approach to the business.

If you can reduce the amount of money you need in order to finance your startup, you will make life simpler. The more money you need, the bigger the stakes in terms of the amount of sales you will need to make, and the more stress you will feel.

The less financing and debt you take on at the beginning, the easier it is to fulfil your obligations to your funders, providing them with a more productive use of their resources. The less money you take, the easier it will be for you to achieve positive cash flow and then profit.

Here are the three most important things to remember about funding:

- Self financing through revenue is by far the best financing there is. It keeps your business focused and maintains your freedom and independence. Whenever you are considering any investment into your business, the most useful question to ask is whether you can finance it through revenue. It may not be possible to rely on revenue alone (it wasn't for me), but the benefits mean it's certainly worth trying.
- Track your cash-flow position as far into the future as possible: it is your early warning system when it comes to financing.

- You probably do not need nearly as much financing as you think. You may even need to run out of money in order to achieve the psychological changes necessary for your growth as a business owner.

CHAPTER SEVEN
# Make Yourself Redundant

*Progress isn't made by early risers. It's made by lazy men trying to find easier ways to do something.*

—Robert A. Heinlein

*If your business depends on you, you don't own a business—you have a job. And it's the worst job in the world because you're working for a lunatic!*

—Michael E. Gerber

At first, I did all the same activities in my own business that I had done in my previous job, but with less pay and more stress! I was involved in every stage of the operation, which made me a single point of failure: if I wasn't there, the business stopped. I had to learn to stop being my own employee within the business and start being an entrepreneur.

Employee conditioning trains you to keep yourself busy, not to be efficient. The assumption is that your job security depends on your employer giving you more and more active responsibilities in the production process. Employees are given as much work as they can take, to the point at which they can barely handle it. The Peter Principle describes this in a funny way: every employee will rise or be promoted to his or her level of incompetence.[20]

In contrast, your fundamental objective as an entrepreneur is to make yourself redundant. This is a completely different way of looking at your role within the business. You *want* to lose your job within the production process as quickly as possible. This is what will make your business efficient and scalable. A successful entrepreneur is a business *owner*, not a business *doer*.[21]

## The Benefits of Making Yourself Redundant

True freedom as an entrepreneur comes when you extract yourself from day-to-day operations. Freedom comes from working *on* your business, not working *in* your business. You gain no freedom from starting a business if you just create a new "job" for yourself, working twice as hard with far more financial risk and stress.

Freedom comes from getting out of the way of your business and removing its dependence on you. Once you can do that, you will be able to take advantage of the autonomy that entrepreneurship brings you, such as being "location independent" and enjoying your own working hours.

Extracting yourself from day-to-day operations not only gives you freedom as an entrepreneur, it also allows your business to *scale*. Extracting yourself means creating a more efficient and scalable business through the creation of standards and procedures. Until you extract yourself, your business may grind to a halt any time you take a holiday or become ill.

Ultimately, the changes that you make in order to extract yourself will become both your competitive advantage and the foundation of your business's value. When you do something efficiently, it's much harder for others to compete with you. You may also want to sell your business one day. This is only possible if you can demonstrate to a buyer that you have created an operation which can survive without you.

Creating an operation that runs independently of you will also reduce the stress involved in the growth of your business. The tasks and tools that will optimize your business are also the things that will enable you to stop firefighting.

This is a virtuous circle: efficiency gains give you more profit, reduce your stress, and give you a competitive advantage—all of which allow you to pursue more efficiency gains.

Let's review what you can do to remove yourself from operational dependency and improve the efficiency of your business.

## Standardization

Standardization is the most basic requirement for creating an operation that is independent of the founder. The aim is to fully define your product or service: determine both the quality standards and delivery specifications. Put simply, this means deciding on one version of each product or service. You decide what you will and won't do, so that you don't have to reinvent it every time you approach a new customer. Everything that you create is easily repeatable because it is so clearly defined.

Standardization doesn't mean that your product never changes. The key is to have standards that everyone in the company knows, even if you keep developing and updating them. You can change product specifications as much as you like as long as you actually have specifications in place. We did this through implementing an operations manual in the form of a Wiki. This provided a great platform with which to update and develop our standards continually.

Standardization also doesn't mean decreeing what you do from above: the more you achieve buy-in on the need for standards from everyone in your operation, the more intelligent your standards are going to be. Everyone who's collaborating in a venture can mutually reinforce the use of standards. By using a Wiki, we enabled everyone in the business to contribute to the development of internal guidelines defining our services and quality standards.

## Proceduralization

Whereas implementing standards means creating one version of each product, implementing *procedures* means creating one method of how you do each particular task. This prevents you from reinventing the wheel every time you do a task. In the case of my business, it meant creating "how to" documents for all the procedures involved in our work, so that we could all agree on them. We defined these collaboratively on our Wiki, with everyone contributing updates.

Proceduralization is the key for quality control. The most basic procedure is simply a checklist of the minimum steps necessary to undertake a task properly. Procedures enable you to capture and maintain the learning that you and your team have accomplished regarding how to produce your product or service to specified quality standards.

Proceduralization allows you to quickly and easily increase production of your products or services. This helps you scale your business: if you need to employ more people they can very quickly get a clear idea of what it is that you do and how you do it, which enables them to become productive much faster.

## Optimization

Optimization means making each of your procedures faster and more efficient. This is done by removing human physical or mental effort from a procedure. If you have a manufacturing procedure that involves physical effort, you can *mechanize* it by using machines to do the work instead. If you have procedures that involve mental effort, you can *automate* it by using computers to do the thinking for you.

In my business, we used software instead of people for as many tasks as possible. We scripted and automated our computing procedures. Many applications have associated scripting languages, which allow the user to automate any series of steps that they regularly perform within the application. For example, we used a type of database called a geographic information system (GIS) that had its own scripting language. Instead of someone having to do repetitive manual tasks on a GIS, we programmed the tasks to happen automatically through a script. Mapping various analyzes was simply a case of pressing a button.

You can script many different kinds of applications and create complex automated procedures, including variables for different outcomes depending on your specific needs each time. We scripted every application that we used intensively and also developed software of our own to automate tasks.

This kind of automation is available to any business that uses computers. The fundamental idea is to remove repetitive drudgery from human work and give it to machines instead. Any time you notice a repetitive procedure, it's a signal that you should try to mechanize or automate it.

There are other opportunities for optimization in things like document templates and reusable content. We made all of the documents that we produced using standard templates with automated formatting. Our reports had to explain the types of analysis that we provided, so we developed reusable content that we could simply paste in.

All of these techniques involve creating faster and more efficient ways to do things you've decided you need to do. This gives you the opportunity to produce more output with the same resources and therefore to generate more profit.

## Knowledge Capture

In designing your business, it's important to accept the fact that any employee or subcontractor may leave at any point. They might encounter more rewarding, exciting or relevant opportunities at any point, no matter what you do as an employer. Hopefully, at some point your employees will try to start businesses for themselves. It's necessary to structure your business taking this into account. This means capturing the knowledge generated by people working for you, so that this knowledge is usable by others later. This idea is known as "knowledge capture."

The key to knowledge capture is avoiding a culture of "gurus" in your business. Just as you don't want your daily operations to be dependent on you as business owner, you also don't want your operations to be dependent on *any* single person. If a guru leaves and takes all their knowledge with them, then you have a real problem. You have to try to work out what on earth that person was doing and rebuild the capability without them.

You can avoid the guru syndrome by getting people to record their knowledge systematically in a form that others can use. This is an integral element of both standardization and proceduralization. If it's part of your company culture that all knowledge is clearly recorded and shared, then the standards and the procedures are in place for new employees. For example, it's important that any IT systems administrators record and share exactly how they are managing your IT systems. That way, if a sysadmin leaves, a new one can see what's been done and can get a handle on everything quickly. To facilitate such transitions, we devoted many pages of our internal Wiki to describing our IT systems in depth.

Even if you have highly skilled employees who are doing things that you don't completely understand, you can still capture the knowledge so that if they leave, you can continue scaling. In this way, you can replace people who leave, without losing a whole chunk of business knowledge along with them.

## Doing the Right Things

One of the traps of optimization is doing senseless tasks more efficiently. It's important not to waste time optimizing activities that are not helping your business. As the famous management consultant Peter Drucker said, "There is nothing so useless as doing efficiently that which should not be done at all." Effective optimization takes place at the level of the business as a whole, not just individual activities. Rather than improving the efficiency of something that you shouldn't be doing, it's better to stop doing it and redirect resources to something more effective or more profitable in the long term.

A vital part of entrepreneurship is the process of *creative destruction*: identifying products and services that don't have a future. The question is, should you really be doing what you are doing? If necessary, you may have to adjust your activities, in order to better fulfill your vision for the business in a way that customers will pay for. This involves taking a step back to ensure that you should be doing any particular activity before investing the time and effort to make it more efficient.

Big corporations find it particularly hard to change their operations because they have built up significant momentum and scale. You have a real advantage as a start-up entrepreneur because you have the flexibility that goes with smaller organizations. Take advantage of this flexibility and get rid of any unnecessary activities as early as possible. The market will force you to make these tough decisions sooner or later anyway and the adjustment will be much harder if it is not at a time of your choosing.

Optimization of your business is intimately related to the "learning by selling" approach discussed in chapter four. If a procedure results in a product or service that nobody will pay for, the optimal choice is to stop doing it and put your energy into something else instead. In my case, that meant stopping the development of an online software application when I learned that our clients actually wanted consultancy services.

## Optimization Makes a Better World

Here are the three most important things to remember about making yourself redundant:

- Extracting yourself from day-to-day operations is essential to your own freedom as an entrepreneur. It is also what allows your business to scale.
- There are three steps to extracting yourself: standardizing your product, creating procedures for all your operations, and optimizing those procedures

- (for example, by using mechanization or automation whenever you see a repetitive process).
- Be careful not to waste time optimizing ultimately senseless activities. It's better to eliminate an activity as soon as you realize that it is commercially unsustainable, rather than waiting until the market forces you to.

Through business optimization, entrepreneurs make the world a better place. This is how economic development happens: *inside* individual firms, driven by business owners. Our lives are improved by the creation of more with less. To see an entrepreneur increasing the efficiency of a business is to see, on a micro-scale, how increases in the overall standard of living actually happen.

In pursuit of optimization, entrepreneurs eliminate repetitive drudgery that people previously had to do. It's one of the most constructive incentives of entrepreneurship: you identify repetitive chores and find ways to get them done more efficiently by a machine instead. This frees up your people and empowers them to focus on what people do best: creative thinking.

CHAPTER EIGHT

# Profit Is Sanity

*Profit tells the entrepreneur that the consumers approve of his ventures; loss, that they disapprove.*

—Ludwig von Mises

Growth is the first order of business for every entrepreneur. When I started my business, I focused exclusively on growth. I had to get everything about the business moving: get sales going, get the operation working, and get people to know that we even existed. I got into the habit of doing whatever it takes to grow, rather than doing whatever it takes to make a profit. I concentrated on growth for so long that when I finally realised that I had to pay more regard to profitability, I had to make difficult adjustments to the business. This chapter is about making the transition to a focus on profit.

Being an employee is bad preparation for understanding profit because "office politics" create distracting incentives. Your primary incentive as an employee is to manage your relationships with your boss and other people in the business. The nature of your role incentivizes you to protect your position rather than focus on profit. If your incentives align so that you are rewarded for contributing to profit without having to worry about office politics, then you work in a well-run business. Unfortunately, that is often not the case.

Managers are also distracted from what matters by the employment system. They are often in a poor position to judge employee performance, but they have to judge it somehow. Many managers end up evaluating staff on the basis of criteria that have little relationship to the ultimate health of the business, like whether an employee is present in the office from nine to five. To make matters worse, they also have to protect their own position within office politics. In this way, everyone ends up focusing on silly things that don't matter. This dysfunctional characteristic of the employee system is so well-known that economists have a term for it: the principal-agent problem.[22]

Breaking free of the employee mentality means getting free of office politics and reconnecting to the most important criteria for judging all work: How effective is it? For the entrepreneur, this is encapsulated in the key concept of profit.

## The Most Intense Feedback You Will Ever Receive

When I first saw financial statements showing whether my business was making a profit or loss, I found it to be some of the most intense feedback that I had ever received. You get the ultimate peer review of both the results of your work and of your methods. Your customers vote with their wallets about whether your product or service is valuable, which tells you whether you have succeeded in making their lives better. Your staff and suppliers also rate your business operation, through the price signals of your expenses.

Together, these combined signals from revenue and expenses will tell you whether you are making losses or profits. If you are making losses, then your business operation is unsustainable. If you are making profits, then what you are doing is sustainable and beneficial to others. This is when you find out just how effective all your efforts have been.

Profit and loss is a more rigorous test than any academic peer-review process. In school and university, at best a few teachers or lecturers evaluate your performance. When you run a business, a vast number of potential customers evaluate your work using their own personal resources. This feedback about your work from so many people provides a challenge that puts you outside your comfort zone, but you only discover your best work through such experiences.

## Vanity Metrics

Many entrepreneurs fall into the trap of pursuing growth at the expense of profitability, as I did. In this mindset, success is usually measured in terms of those things that show growth: revenue, page views, Twitter followers, etc. The problem comes when these growth metrics ignore profit. Often growth is measured by expense metrics, such as the employee headcount. This is the most dangerous way of all to measure your success.

This emphasis on growth leads you to measure your success by so-called *vanity metrics*: measures of growth, not profit.[23] You can also see this in the corporate world, where people define success as the number of *warm bodies* that work in your business unit or your division of the corporation.

For many business managers, the measure of success ultimately comes down to the size of their fiefdom. Managers who think like this aspire to build an empire, not make a profit. They often get positive reinforcement for this attitude from the people that they meet. New acquaintances commonly ask them how many employees work for them. A large headcount is considered impressive in corporate life. In contrast, managers are very rarely asked how profitable their business unit is.

Although it's dangerous for a business to become obsessed with growth, there are strong incentives pushing you towards growth at the expense of profit. The main one is the tax system: the fact that profit is taxed creates a strong incentive to preempt taxes by investing any potential profit into company growth. Corporations grow big partly because the tax system fundamentally disincentivizes profitability and incentivizes growth.

The tax system also incentivizes solo entrepreneurs to minimize profit. Your tax bill gets less onerous as you claim more expenses, which encourages you to push the maximum allowable expenses through the business. This can warp your strategy and lead you to lose sight of what is best for the business.

## Profit is Sanity

An advisor told me a great saying about profit while we were discussing how to value my business. He said, "Revenue is vanity and profit is sanity." What a striking and succinct way of explaining profit! Many people value their businesses in terms of how big they are or how many people they employ, but the *rational* value of a business is its profitability. The pursuit of profit is the best guiding light for the health of your business.

If you don't have the profit motive, I guarantee that your expenses will rise to match or outpace your sales—that's a law of nature. Adopting the profit motive will enable you to keep expenses in check and make money; otherwise, you will be so involved in the excitement of growth that your expenses will always match any money you make.

The profit motive will stop you from falling into the same trap that I did. In the first couple of years, I struggled to get my business going. We did projects "at cost," just to get something under our belts so that we could demonstrate our capabilities to our customers. It was the right approach for a while: gradually we started to get more and more projects, each one bigger than the last. Then we got a huge project, so we hired more people and moved to a bigger office. We spent all our money keeping up with the growth opportunity. Everything seemed to be going well.

Before we knew it, we were so involved in delivering the increased workload that we weren't making enough sales, weren't making a profit, and had no cash reserves. Once our biggest project ended, our revenue fell off a cliff. We had to make some difficult and painful decisions, including laying off staff.

After that shock, I made a deliberate attitude shift from focusing on growth to focusing on profit. With all the decisions I faced about the business (what to spend money on, how to develop our services, etc.), I used profitability as a guide. The first step was making that mental change.

## Tracking Expenses

The second step towards profitability was rather obvious, but nonetheless difficult: we had to cut our expenses to significantly less than our revenue so that we had a bigger profit margin. It's so simple that it's almost silly to mention, but this is where the rubber meets the road if one is to make a profit. The question is, how to do it? The answer comes back to the tracking and analysis of business intelligence discussed in chapter five.

We had to analyze our business expenses regularly and in detail, in order to control them. I hired an advisor who helped us get into the habit of critically reviewing all our expenses on a regular basis. For each line item, we asked ourselves "Why are we spending money on this? What is it for? Do we really need it?"

In the excitement of entrepreneurship and growth, you can find yourself spending money on things that you simply don't need. If there is more than one founder, you also have a responsibility to be conscious of what each of you is spending. It was useful to get an outside perspective and to effectively audit every single expense involved in the business. It helped us assess whether we really needed each item. I became far more conscious about what we were spending money on as a consequence.

## Tracking Time as an Expense

Human time is usually the most significant business expense. If your business charges by time, then a detailed tracking of time spent is essential for billing purposes. However, even if you have a product-based business, your time is still your ultimate scarce resource. Therefore, tracking it is essential if you want to analyze your profitability. You need to track time as an expenditure in order to get transparency on how you are spending it.

Everyone hates filling in timesheets, but you can now automate the collection of this kind of data to a large extent. If you use an app that tracks what you are doing on your computer in the background, you can then specify which documents or applications apply to which projects and get an automated time utilization analysis.

You can also facilitate time tracking within a task-planning app, so tracking is not simply additional administrative overhead for the user. I had a task database developed for my company which we used it to plan and track individual projects in real time, so we always knew at the end of each week how much time we'd spent on any particular project. This data not only underpinned the profitability analysis that we did at the project level; it also informed staff evaluations and my own time planning.

## Operational Profitability

It is extremely useful to have a database of metrics relating to the profitability of your different business activities. Whether your business has different products, services, projects, or any combination of the three, you need to know how much profit margin each activity is contributing to the business. The technical term for this is the *contribution margin*.

The profit margin of each business activity shows you which activities are worth doing more and which are not worth doing at all. This helps you guide the business into those more profitable areas and decide what to do about unprofitable activities.

What you track will depend on your type of business. For example, in our business, we assessed the profitability of each consulting *project*.[24] We subtracted all project-related expenses from the project fee in order to calculate the profit margin that each project contributed to the business. Then we compared projects of different kinds, splitting the data by every characteristic that we thought might be important (e.g., type, size, sector, client, etc.).

We tracked all the time spent on every stage of every project. That enabled us to identify which *kinds* of projects made money and which lost them and even which stages of projects made or lost money.

The results of our profitability analysis were not what we expected and led us to change our approach in many ways. It prompted us to ask ourselves why we were doing some types of work that made us no money, when we could be doing more of other types of work that brought in all the profit.

Much of what I imagined would be profitable was proved wrong by the data. For example, I learned just how dangerous big projects could be. They look great because they seem to promise economies of scale and secured revenue for a long time. In fact, it can be very difficult to control costs on big projects. Their size makes it harder to estimate costs accurately up front. The project scope and client expectations are also harder to manage. The bigger the project, the more careful I had to be about estimating fees and controlling costs.

## Beyond Vanity

Here are the three most important points to remember about profit:

- Every entrepreneur has to make the transition from the initial pursuit of growth to the conscious pursuit of profit.
- If you don't adopt the profit motive, your expenses will rise to match or outpace your sales and you won't make any money.
- Only by adopting rigorous tracking and analysis will you know where your profit comes from. You are unlikely to get to profitability unless you implement sufficient tracking to give you this information.

Many imagine that the profit motive is a distraction from doing great work. They see it as something that turns good people into mindless profit-chasing automatons. Of course, some people lack ethics and are willing to do anything for a profit. But that is not how the profit motive works for me, nor for the majority of entrepreneurs whom I've seen.

Profit is a guiding light that tells you whether or not your customers approve of what you are doing. Such intense feedback can be humbling. *Revenue is vanity and profit is sanity.* Doing your best work means getting beyond your vanity to create something authentically useful. I have found that using profitability to direct my efforts is the best way to move my work closer to the best work that it can be.

CHAPTER NINE
# JFDI (Just Fucking Do It)

*The world can only be grasped by action, not by contemplation. The hand is more important than the eye ... The hand is the cutting edge of the mind.*

—Joseph Bronowski

*There's tremendous power in putting your ass where your heart wants to be.*

—Stephen Pressfield

It's easy to appreciate the idea of becoming an entrepreneur; it's harder to plunge into the exhilarating free fall of doing it. One of the worst legacies of our conditioning is the inability to see the opportunity in risk and unpredictability. We've been trained to look for jobs that give us predictability.

The fact is that when you get started in business, you have no control over the opportunity flow. You can prepare as much as you like, but it will be totally different as soon as you get started. Every business is created in uncertainty. You never know for sure if it will work beforehand and you never know exactly how you will do it. As the science-fiction author Ray Bradbury put it, you *jump off a cliff and build wings on the way down.*

At some point, you have to confront paralysis, indecision, and procrastination in order to create anything in the face of uncertainty. Starting a business requires you to risk failure in order to achieve something truly remarkable.

It is not lack of preparation that holds people back from starting their own businesses; it is that they haven't given themselves permission. Ultimately, the way that I broke my employee conditioning was by giving myself permission to act outside it.

## Permission to Risk Failure

If you're going to start a business, it's essential to give yourself permission to risk failure. Do you even allow yourself this option? If you're not willing to contemplate it, you'll never get started.

One of the biggest breaks I gave myself when I started a business was permission to risk it all being a big flop. I made a commitment to myself: I would build the business for five years. I decided that if I had not created something of value by that point, then I would just give up and get a job. If I failed, I would still have a great experience in trying. After five years, we had paid off all our debts and become profitable, so I knew that the business had real value. Two years later, we sold the company.

The people who really matter to you are going to respect you much more for having gone for it and thrown your passion into your venture, even if you then discover that you miscalculated the opportunity. They will respect you much more if you try and fail than if you never follow your dream. *You* will respect yourself much more if you go for it than if you never risk it.

Let's travel ahead in time a couple of years from now. Imagine that this is what has happened: you started the business of your dreams. You took the plunge and ... failed spectacularly. You burned up your savings. You called in your favors. You threw your heart and soul into it and you were greeted by indifference ... the sound of crickets. Nobody wanted what you had to sell. After a couple of years, embarrassed, you gave up. You ceased trading.

Even if such a worst-case scenario happened, would it really be bad for you? Even if your business were to fail, you would have the fulfillment and satisfaction of someone who dared greatly. Unrealised dreams will not haunt you. You will never look back on your life and wonder whether that venture would have succeeded had you tried. You will know that, unlike the vast majority, you had the courage to risk failure and to create something you believed in. But you will also gain far more.

Starting a business is the best business education that money can buy. It teaches you far more than acquiring an MBA ever could, regardless of the outcome. You will learn more by creating a business than you could ever hope to learn by reading about other people who did it (or, even worse, reading the theories of bystanders who have never even tried). You'd probably have to spend far more money paying off student debts from doing an MBA than you would ever burn in starting a business that failed. As long as you allow yourself to learn from the experience, a failed business will stand you in fantastic stead for the next venture. You can choose not to make the same mistakes again.

Even if it fails, you can always get a job afterwards if you need to, or you can start another business. Your life will be richer from the experience because, unlike most, at least you dared to try.

## Permission to Be Imperfect

Another thing that really holds people back in starting a business is perfectionism. Many people say to themselves, "I will start trading, but I just need to get this and that right first. I'm going to get my logo done and website redesigned. I don't want to make a bad impression, so I'm not ready to launch yet." That state of mind can go on for years.

It's never going to be just right. There are always going to be things that you think you could improve about your business. It's always going to be imperfect, and that is OK because the most important thing is to get launched and start trading. As Reid Hoffman has put it, if version 1.0 isn't embarrassing to you, then you're launching too late.[25]

Resist the temptation to wait until you are so well prepared that you are completely unassailable to criticism. That day will never come. It does not serve you to believe that you can make something so damn good that nobody is going to be able to criticize it. Of course, you're always going to have people criticizing what you're doing. Haters gonna hate! Give yourself permission to be imperfect.

When I started, I couldn't read accounts. I didn't have any clients. I couldn't properly describe the service that we were providing because I was confused about the purpose of my business. The point is, I started. I made contact with the marketplace. This was the best teacher of all; it was how I learned what my business was for. Through the embarrassment of starting imperfectly, I realized what needed changing. I created a business that was worth a lot because I dared to start trading when it was worth nothing.

## Permission to Make Waves

Entrepreneurs are often seen as a pain in the ass because they want to bring something new into the world, which also means that they don't accept the world as it is. They want to change the way other people think and live, which also means that they think they know better. They don't stick with received wisdom, which means that they are fundamentally disruptive. All this can be very annoying to other people.

Giving yourself permission to make waves is vital. Starting a business will inevitably involve annoying people. Every time you try to change the world in any significant way, you will displease somebody. If you believe that risking the annoyance of other people is out of the question, then you will seriously hinder your progress.

I am not suggesting that you should give yourself license to do anything unprincipled. Giving yourself permission to make waves does not mean giving yourself permission to betray your values. However, even when you stick to your ethics, by starting a business you will still annoy the competition because they won't want you to enter their marketplace. You may upset a whole bunch of other people too.

Every transition that I have made in business has annoyed some people. After I finished my PhD, I had the opportunity to continue working within the consulting unit at my university. I tried it for a while, but realized I wanted to start my own company. I decided to leave university, take what I had learned, and apply it in the real world. Some professors in the university were very annoyed by my decision. Understandably, they wanted me to stay at the university and they didn't want me to compete with them in the marketplace. I didn't take any of their clients when I left and I did nothing ethically wrong by competing in the market. Nonetheless, my leaving disrupted the plans they had for me and for their business. This made them angry. If I hadn't been willing to accept that the consequences of my actions might upset them, then I wouldn't have been able to start my own business.

Perhaps you will be better at minimizing the number of people whom you upset when you start a business. Many people are better at diplomacy and have better people skills than I had. I might have avoided annoying people if I'd handled things differently. However, even if you handle it far better than I did, I still truly believe that you're going to have to give yourself permission to do things that make some people angry, because if you don't, it will hold you back.

Give yourself permission to upset people, if the choice is between that and not launching. Don't be prevented from doing what you truly believe in just because some people will be pissed off.

## Permission to Succeed

The biggest barrier for many people is the one they can't admit to themselves: they haven't given themselves permission to succeed. It was a big deal for me to admit to myself that I wanted to succeed. I wanted financial independence. I found it scary to admit that I wanted to make my fortune and to be able to do whatever I wanted in life.

If you want to become an entrepreneur, I recommend that you abandon the idea of testing the waters or seeing how it goes. That will not serve you. Instead, I encourage you to desire it with every fiber in your being; to be completely committed to doing your absolute best to make your venture a wild success.

This is a vulnerable thing to admit to yourself: that you dearly want to succeed. It often puts you up against a lot of the conditioning that you have undergone in school and with your family. We are conditioned to fit in, to be acceptable, to be part of the crowd. Success interferes with this conditioning. When you allow yourself to succeed, you no longer conform. I believe that the most important permission that you can give yourself is permission to succeed.

## JFDI in Life

The best way to summarize my final suggestion is with the acronym JFDI; in other words, Just Fucking Do It. This is what the experience of entrepreneurship teaches us about life. Living is expressed in action, not contemplation. A thought that does not lead to action somewhere down the line is useless, except for the gratification it brings in the moment. It doesn't *get* you anywhere. Yes, we all need to stop and smell the roses sometimes, but that is consumption, not creativity.

The only way to be creative is to act. If you really take this knowledge on board, it frees you enormously. If you want to make anything, action is always better than inaction, no matter how imperfect you think the result is. Our conditioning has left us with the fear that starting a business is as risky as jumping off a cliff, but the biggest cliff is the one in your mind. Jump off the cliff and build your wings on the way down. It's scary at first, but once you are airborne, it is a wonderful adventure.

# Further Resources

If you enjoyed this book, please help me out by leaving a review on Amazon. Thanks!

I talk about all the aspects of entrepreneurship covered in this book, and much more besides, on my podcast The Voluntary Life. You can subscribe to the podcast at thevoluntarylife.com. To see all previous episodes on entrepreneurship, go to thevoluntarylife.com/search/label/entrepreneurship.

To get updates about upcoming books and podcasts, please join my email update list at this link: bit.ly/tvlmail.

# Further Reading

Allen, David. *Getting Things Done: The Art of Stress-Free Productivity*. New York: Penguin Books, 2001.

Allen, David. *Making It All Work: Winning at the Game of Work and the Business of Life*. New York: Penguin Books, 2009.

Branson, Richard. *Losing My Virginity*. London: Virgin Books, 1999.

Covey, Stephen. *The Seven Habits of Highly Effective People: Powerful Lessons in Personal Change*. New York: RosettaBooks, 2013.

Fisher, Roger and William Ury *Getting to Yes: Negotiating Agreement Without Giving In*. 2$^{nd}$ ed. New York: Penguin Books, 1991.

Gerber, Michael E. *The E-myth Revisited: Why Most Small Businesses Don't Work and What to Do About It*. New York: HarperCollins, 1995.

Graham, Paul. "The 18 Mistakes that Kill Startups." October 2006. http://www.paulgraham.com/startupmistakes.html.

Fried, Jason and David Heinemeier Hansson. *ReWork: Change the Way You Work Forever*. New York: Vermilion, 2010.

Hopkins, Tom. *How to Master the Art of Selling*. New York: HarperCollins, 1981.

Kawasaki, Guy. *The Art of the Start: The Time-Tested, Battle-Hardened Guide for Anyone Starting Anything*. New York: Portfolio, 2004.

Mises, Ludwig von. *Profit and Loss*. Auburn: Ludwig Von Mises Institute, 2008.

Pink, Dan. *Drive: The Surprising Truth About What Motivates Us*. New York: Penguin Books, 2009.

Ries, Eric. *The Lean Startup: How Today's Entrepreneurs Use Continuous Innovation to Create Radically Successful Businesses*. New York: Crown Business, 2011.

Sivers, Derek. *Anything You Want*. Amazon, 2011.

# Acknowledgements

I am grateful to all the people who helped me create this book. Hannah Braime and Matt Amberson both read more drafts of the manuscript than I can remember. Their valuable feedback helped me shape the book. The following people also kindly read drafts of the manuscript and provided valuable feedback: Alan, András Gosztonyi, Angela Gross, Brett Veinotte, C.S. Runberg, Carlos Massiah, Chris Robinson, Daniel Mackler, David Adkins, David Albrecht, Emily Crotteau, Geoffrey Allan Plauché, George Grigoropoulos, Harry Penner, Ib Vegger, Jacea Yecker, Jacob M. Ramirez, James Walpole, Kristov Widak, Matt H., Michael DeMarco, Michael January, Mike Mitcham, Phoenix Zerin, Roger Browne, Sarah Burch, Stefan Ogden, Stephen Adkins, Steve Miller-Miller, Theresa Carter, Thomas Bell, Tim Lee, and Zsolt Babocsai. Responsibility for the content and any errors in the book is mine.

I am grateful to all the people who worked with me over the years of the founding growth and sale of Intelligent Space. I would like to mention a few specifically, in chronological order. My father Justin encouraged me to start the business and was supportive during the trials of startup. Paul B.W. gave encouragement, lent me a lot of money, and trusted that I would pay him back. Elspeth Finch was a trustworthy and resolute business partner who brought inspiring energy, determination, and good will through all the challenges we faced together. Keith Harris wrote brilliant software and was a good friend to me during difficult times. Frank Hebbert contributed much to the business at a crucial stage. András Gosztonyi provided amazing expertise which helped turn the business around and was a good friend to me in difficult times. Peter Drown was the best advisor I could have wished for during one of the most important negotiations of my life. Farshid Kamali and Andy Southern made the eventual sale of Intelligent Space possible. Responsibility for all the mistakes I made becoming an entrepreneur is mine.

# About the Author

Jake Desyllas is the host of *The Voluntary Life,* a podcast about entrepreneurship, financial independence, and freedom. In 2000, he founded *Intelligent Space*, an award-winning consultancy that led innovation in the field of pedestrian movement simulation and analysis. In 2010, he sold his business, quit the rat race, and retired early at the age of thirty-eight.

He has a bachelors degree, a masters degree, and a doctorate. He is dedicated to promoting entrepreneurship both as an effective personal liberation program that is available to everyone, and as a peaceful method of solving social problems. He is a perpetual traveler, a minimalist, a Getting Things Done (GTD) enthusiast, an avid reader of philosophy and psychology, and a marathon inline skater.

[19] Indiegogo, http://www.indiegogo.com.

[20] "Peter Principle," Wikipedia, last modified March 17, 2014, https://en.wikipedia.org/wiki/Peter_principle.

[21] The best book I have read on the idea of making yourself redundant is Michael E. Gerber's *The E-myth Revisited: Why Most Small Businesses Don't Work and What to Do About It* (New York: HarperCollins, 1995).

[22] "Principal-Agent Problem, Wikipedia, last modified March 17, 2014, https://en.wikipedia.org/wiki/Principal-agent_problem.

[23] More discussion of vanity metrics can be found in Eric Ries, *The Lean Startup: How Today's Entrepreneurs Use Continuous Innovation to Create Radically Successful Businesses* (Crown Business, 2011).

[24] If you have a product-based business, you can do the same on a product basis.

[25] "How LinkedIn's Founder Got Started," interview of Reid Hoffman by Alyssa Abkowitz, August 25, 2009, http://money.cnn.com/2009/08/24/technology/linkedin_reid_hoffman.fortune/index.htm.

Made in the USA
Charleston, SC
15 October 2014